YOU DON'T HEAR ME COMPLAINING

BRIAN CONROY

For Wren
who always listens

TABLE OF CONTENTS

WHITE MEN
CAN'T DANCE

E VERY TIME I HEAR MARVIN Gaye, I start bustin' moves. Killer moves. Turn on some Smokey Robinson, some Jackie Wilson, The Marvelettes, and I can't stand still. The ground beneath my feet becomes a dance floor and I'm gone. If I didn't have white skin, you'd think I was black.

Twenty years ago, my wife, Wren, would join me on our makeshift dance floor — in the kitchen, the hallway, the living room. I'd curl a suggestive finger in her direction and we'd revert to adolescence, twisting the night away to Sam Cooke. Today, she just rolls her eyes and finds something urgent to attend to in the other room.

She tells me to take a good look at myself in the mirror. So I do. I whip out my best moves in front of the bathroom mirror, like I used to do before junior high dances. And there's my proof. I still got it, baby!

So I boogaloo down Broadway to where Wren is pretending to read a book. She tries to fake an embarrassed expression, but she knows she wants some of my fine stuff. I guess when you got it all going on it can be kind of intimidating for your loved ones. I get it.

I mean, check me out. With my smooth moves, I belong on Soul Train. Yeah, I'm hip that Soul Train's been off the air for, like, ten years, but you dig what I mean. It wouldn't work out anyway, cause the next time Bruno Mars bounces into town, he's gonna sign me as the token white dude in his group. Once he checks me getting my groove on, he'll start closing his shows with a dance-off between us two playas. I can see it now: Bruno and Brian. Say what?

People always ask me, Yo, B-dog, how'd you get so jiggy wit' it? I let 'em in on a little secret. I dance like no one's watching. But Wren insists someone *is* watching. She is. These days she evaluates my dancing like a judge on *So You Think You Can Dance*. She insists that when I dance, I launch into the white man's overbite thing that Billy Crystal taught the world in the movie *When Harry Met Sally*. Ouch! Where's the love? I don't even *have* an overbite. That thing she's talking about, that's just being sassy.

Wren sees that gleam in my eye and knows what's coming, so she makes a quick getaway. Not quick enough, though. I'm on her heels like a soul stalker, doin' The Swim straight into the kitchen. In front of the refrigerator, she reminds me that I'm white. I tell her I got soul, baby. That soul transcends skin color. Besides, I tell her, I have black friends. But she points out that just because Jamal, who bags our groceries at Whole Foods, calls me "bro" doesn't make him my "friend." I remind her of the time I danced the soles off one of my shoes at her best friend's wedding reception. Wren cites that as evidence that I don't have *any* soul—at least on one foot. She's a real comedian.

I recount the story of winning first place in a junior high dance contest, dancing with my first crush to *Love Child* by The Supremes. But I figure, talk is cheap. Actions speak louder than words. So I start to walk the talk. *Moon*walk, that is. Oh, it's on now! I throw down mad skills that make The Gloved One look like a member of The Partridge

Family. How many white dudes can do that, I ask her. She tells me to put the white glove back in the garage with the garden tools.

Wren's clearly not buying my rap. When things get to this point, I take it to another level. I know it's not playing fair, but I go to my main man, Barry White. I dust off one of Wren's favorite CDs, turn up the volume, and press play.

Can't get enough of your love, babe...

Oh, yeah. Now that's my jam! I be getting down with my bad self. The temperature in the kitchen heats up. There's nothing on the stove, but I be cookin'. I curl an inviting finger toward Wren. Only this time she doesn't run into the living room looking for her knitting. I knew the girl could only resist for so long. She shakes a hip, which turns to a shimmy. Then her hand starts swinging back and forth at her side. Her eyes close and she's gone, dancing like no one's watching.

Me? I'm on the good foot. Got my mojo working. Lettin' my backbone slip with my funky hip chick. Hey, I may not be black, but with Barry White putting us in the mood, for three slammin' minutes, I am her Soul Brother Number One.

SHOP TILL YOU DROP

MACHINES HATE ME. THEY KNOW I've never loved them. So whenever they see me coming, they cop an attitude and start breaking down. It never fails—cars, computers, appliances. They sense my mechanical ineptitude. I have a long, complicated history with all things that go whirr. Apparently they've never forgiven me for betraying them in my youth.

Not long after my father died, my well-intentioned mother got it in her head that without a dad to show me around a toolbox, I wouldn't survive in this cruel, mechanical world. So in junior high and high school, Mom insisted I take every shop class that was offered.

"Hey, Mom, can I take Public Speaking this year?"

"You kidding? You talk too much as it is. You're taking Machine Shop."

"Machine Shop?! They don't even have Machine Shop."

"I don't care. You're taking it!"

As if the onset of adolescence wasn't degrading enough, as soon as puberty kicked in, I was subjected to the humiliation of three consecutive years of Wood Shop, Metal Shop and Auto Shop. But Mom was only looking out for my best interests. She had the foresight to know that there would be job security in places like Flint, Michigan or Detroit in the burgeoning auto industry. She had heard they were hiring high school graduates who had taken Machine Shop.

5

In the fall of 1970, while the world was awakening to the dawning of the Age of Aquarius, to flower power and personal liberation, I was imprisoned in Auto Shop with the cast of *Lord of the Flies*. Don't get me wrong. I had nothing against my classmates. They seemed nice enough. It's just that we were not members of the same species. They were still perfecting the art of walking upright. On the evolutionary chart, they were the figure second from the left. Nor had they mastered the complexities of language, communicating instead through a series of monosyllabic grunts and groans. Their preferred method of communication was kinesthetic, tending toward pushing, shoving and grab-ass in favor of verbal expression.

When you get that many high school neanderthals together in an enclosed space, no good can come of it. A tribal mentality pervades the atmosphere. A strict pecking order emerges. As one of the shortest kids in shop class, and the least familiar with tools, I found myself at the bottom of the pecking order. A scrawny chicken in a coop full of cocks. I knew I had to fly the coop before all that was left of me was feathers.

The Auto Shop teacher was a thick-necked specimen named Mr. Pimentel, who resembled a bouncer at a longshoreman's bar. His woeful lack of pedagogical skills was likely the reason he had never been awarded Teacher of the Year. He barked out his class lectures like a drill sergeant, sneering contemptuously at the mental midgets who were his cross to bear. The threat of pushups for the hapless saps who weren't listening with rapt attention to his enthralling lectures, hung constantly in the air.

One morning he held aloft a carburetor.

"All right, ladies, listen up. This here is a carburetor. Our first class project will be to rebuild a carburetor." My classmates began to ooh and ahh, their eyes glazed over in automotive bliss.

"In case you geniuses weren't aware, automobiles run on an internal combustion engine. That combustion depends on the proper mixture of air and gas." The pituitary case next to me made a fart sound and pointed at me when Pimentel glared in our direction. But not even artificial flatulence could deter Pimentel when he was on a roll. "A carburetor is the mechanism that blends air and fuel to create that combustion. Any questions so far?"

No one dared raise a hand, for fear of sounding stupid.

For the next twenty minutes Pimentel droned on about inlet manifolds, choke valves, accelerator pump diaphragms, fuel pressure regulators and secondary throttle diaphragms. With every new component he introduced, some witty horndog would find sexual innuendo in the term, and perform a lewd gesture for the benefit of his oversexed pals.

"Now, I'm gonna give each of you young ladies your own carb. Your job is to take it apart and rebuild it. Any questions?"

Yeah, I thought. What the hell am I doing here? What have I done to deserve this punishment? Can't you see I don't belong here? I'm an artist. I wasn't meant to work with tools. Somebody transfer me! Quick! Before I mutate into a gear head!

The next day I scheduled an appointment with the guidance counselor, Mr. Duffy. Those were the days when counselors wanted to be on the same wavelength as their students. They tried to act hip. They wore tight bellbottoms. They carried man bags. Duffy couldn't be more accommodating. He told me he could easily make the transfer. All I had to do was get my mom's signature. Damn! I knew there was a catch.

It took a week's worth of sweet talk and persuasion, combined with extra chores and an onslaught of compliments, until Mom finally broke down and agreed to let me transfer out of Auto Shop. Her natural assumption was that I would transfer to Wood Shop or AV, or at least Home Ec. When I told her my first choice would be Choir, there were tears in her eyes.

"Choir?!" she gasped, crestfallen. She took it personally. She felt she had failed as a parent. To her it was a slippery slope. She was convinced it was merely a matter of time before I would be wearing dresses and playing with dolls. This was the moment she hoped she would never have to face. Her son was a singer.

Early the next morning, with trembling fingers, I returned the signed transfer form to Mr. Duffy, and was liberated from Auto Shop forever.

Later that day, I breezed into my new elective. The music room was overflowing with earth goddesses, writers for the literary magazine, nerds, loners, thespians and Friends of Dorothy. I fit right in.

Mrs. Valenti, the free-spirited Choir instructor, started us off with a tune by Carole King: *It's Gonna Take Some Time*. Yes, it's gonna take some time, but what a way to spend my time.

I've been singing ever since.

LIKE A ROLLING STONE

T HE MOON HAD SKIPPED TOWN, and it didn't leave a forwarding address. The streetlights were hungover, sleeping off last night's bender. When no one was watching, some Jackson Pollock wannabe splattered black paint across the sky, making the downtown streets safe for crooks and thugs. In the city that never sleeps, the only ones catching a snooze tonight were the boys in blue.

I was shuffling down a dark walkway in Washington Square Park, trying to avoid getting mugged. Out of the shadows, a hooded figure emerged, and fell in step with me. I glanced askance at him, so he couldn't tell I was eyeballing him. He shot a quick look at me, did a double take, and blurted, "Damn, you look like one of The Rolling Stones."

My confidence surged, as I strolled with a little more cut to my strut. This big city cat thinks I look like one of The Stones. We're talking about the coolest rock stars on the planet. But then, maybe he meant I'm old and washed up. After all, The Stones are all in their seventies. In concert, they hide behind lighting and pyrotechnics that make them appear young and agile. At their mansions, they limp around with walkers and canes. When they're not in the public eye, their wardrobes consist of Depends and orthopedic shoes. The only way they can get "satisfaction" these days is by taking increasingly larger doses of Viagra.

That's the price they have to pay to maintain their status as hardened rock stars.

"The Stones are all, like, seventy years old," I point out to my newest friend.

He disregards this as irrelevant information, and speaks at a rate he feels a sixty-year-old brain can follow. "You know who I mean, right?"

"The drummer who has white hair and is almost eighty?"

"No, the other one."

"You mean, the bass player who married a fifteen-year-old?"

"No, man, the other guy. What's his name?"

"The drug addict with all the wrinkles?...The guy with the big lips?"

"Naw, naw. Man, you white people are supposed to know these things! What's the guy's name with the hair?"

"Oh! Ron Wood?"

"Yeah, that's the guy. You look just like him."

Turns out this is the third time I've been mistaken for Ron Wood. It could be that I dress flamboyantly, with bright scarves and headbands, though that's unlikely. Woody and I do share similar European features—high cheekbones, deep wrinkles, an angular jaw, a prominent nose. But I think our strongest similarity is that both of us still have a full head of hair. Ronnie dyes his; mine is natch. I'm not saying I have great hair like Ron Wood's, but I do have hair; something that's uncommon in men our age.

So I can understand perfectly how a dude who never listens to rock music, staggering through the darkness of a moonless night, would mistake me for Ron Wood. Hell, at least he didn't think I was Elton John. In a place like Manhattan where everybody looks like somebody, it's nice to be recognized, even if it's mistakenly.

I continued on through a seedy section of the park, past prowlers and pickpockets, affecting a Cockney accent, playing up my new found fame for all it was worth. My latest buddy swerved left, bursting with bragging rights. As I turned in the other direction I heard him shout out to a partner in crime, "Yo, I just saw one of The Rolling Stones."

"Which one? The junkie with the wrinkles?"

"No, man, the other one."

"The one with the big lips?"

"Naw, naw..."

The windows of the nearby brownstones scowled down at the sidewalk. In the distance I heard a voice rising in the Manhattan night, "Check it! Is that Beyonce over there?"

NATTY IN A NEHRU

MAN, YOU SHOULD HAVE DUG me in 1968 on my thirteenth birthday. There I was, decked out in the swankiest birthday present ever: a powder blue Nehru jacket. I looked like a rock star. There was no denying it. I was making a fashion statement. Natty in a Nehru.

In case you're not hip, the Nehru was wildly popular for about five minutes during the late 60s. It's a kind of collarless Indian sports coat with a notch cut out at the neck, under which a dickie is worn. Nehru jackets were named after India's first prime minister, Pundit Jawaharlal Nehru, who ironically, never wore one. Go figure. But all four Beatles dressed in matching Nehrus when they played Shea Stadium. The Monkees wore them on that episode where they pretended to be hippies. Sean Connery sported one as James Bond in the movie *Dr. No*. And I wore mine to the spring dance when I was in eighth grade. Oh yeah!

Now, if you think that the 1969 spring dance at Samuel Curtis Rogers Junior High was trivial, you were never an adolescent. Talk about timing. On the precise evening of the spring dance, I was at the pinnacle of puberty. A late comer to the puberty party, I made up for lost time by producing enough hormonal energy in the first months of my thirteenth year to power a banana republic. In three months, my voice changed from soprano to baritone, acne ravaged my skin so that my face resembled a combination pizza, and I was randy as a rabbit and ready to hop.

If you've inferred that I was some kind of sex-crazed maniac, you must be psychic. It's true I was what clinical psychologists refer to as "chronically horny." Yet, I was not to blame for the puerile thoughts that dominated my consciousness. I believe I can sum up the source of my distraction in a single word: mini skirt.

During that golden year of 1968-1969, everywhere you looked on campus (and believe me, I did), girls were rocking mini skirts. Girls flaunted their new found liberation by wearing shorter and shorter skirts. Females had come a long way, baby, and as a thirteen-year-old stalker, I had taken notice. I was witnessing history up close and personal. And I liked what I saw. I saw more thigh that year than a fry cook at KFC.

Early in the year, the school administration adopted a laissez-faire approach to mini skirt lengths. The times they were a-changing, they reasoned. What harm could a mini skirt pose to a libidinous adolescent? But as the school year progressed, school nurses noted a sharp increase in hypertension among male students that seemed to manifest only during break and lunch. When administrators observed an inordinate number of boys' tongues hanging below their chins every time a mini-skirted girl passed by, they knew it was time for a more hands-on approach to mini skirts.

In January, a committee of concerned faculty convened to address the controversy. After a heated discussion, the wording of the school dress code was amended to: "Skirt lengths shall be no shorter than six inches from hemline to kneecap."

One of the strictest teachers in the school, Madeleine Blatinich, declared it her personal mission to combat the scourge of mini skirts. She raved that the damned, skimpy things were a symptom of a larger problem, which would lead to the deterioration of society's morals, and a devaluing of academic standards. (Research failed to corroborate her assessment, as school attendance had never been so high, especially among boys.) To the great admiration of the school's principal, Mrs. Blatinich resolved to stand in the hallways before school and be ever vigilant in her quest to eradicate mini skirt infractions.

The following Monday, Mrs. Blatinich took up her post in the central corridor of the school, wielding a wooden ruler. When she saw a girl wearing a skirt that appeared shorter than regulation length, Blatinich would slap a cold ruler onto the girl's knee and extend it up the girl's thigh to her hemline. If the hem was in excess of six inches from the knee, the girl would be unceremoniously escorted to the office, where she would be forced to change into something more suitable.

Boys considered the practice inhumane. Not because it was degrading or violated a girl's civil rights. To us, the flesh of an inner thigh was one of the natural wonders of the world, and therefore unconscionable to cover up. At this rate, we would have to revert to using our imaginations to satisfy our dirty minds. Girls forced to endure Blatinich's humiliation, took a sudden interest in the practice of voodoo. At home, they named their dolls Madeleine, accessorized them with miniature rulers, and jabbed pins in the dolls' eyes. When Mrs. Blatinich arrived at school one day wearing glasses, they knew they were on to something. But the glasses only enhanced Blatinich's skill for sizing up an exposed thigh.

That spring, the school was infected with an outbreak of spring fever. When the date of the spring dance was announced, every pubescent creep in the school anxiously awaited what they hoped would be the evening of their lives. The word spread that Mrs. Blatinich would not be one of the chaperones at the spring dance. In a show of solidarity, dozens of girls vowed to wear their shortest mini skirts. I vowed to wear my powder blue Nehru jacket.

Full disclosure: this was going to be the very first time I'd worn the Nehru in public. Though I'd gotten the jacket the previous October, there weren't a ton of opportunities to wear a Nehru jacket in my neighborhood. It wasn't exactly standard school wear. If I wore the jacket to my little league games, I'd be setting myself up for endless abuse. At church, they'd think I was trying to mock the priest and I'd risk excommunication. But at the spring dance, a Nehru would be cooler than a popsicle on ice.

On the night of the dance, I buttoned my Nehru impeccably, slicked down my cowlick, splashed on some Old Spice, and made the scene. Inside the gymnasium of Samuel Curtis Rogers Junior High, the lights were dimmed low, so that it was difficult to notice the cluster of zits festering on my chin. Surveying the crowd, I scoped out the bevy of bodacious babes wearing mini skirts. But I quickly realized there was only one dude wearing a Nehru jacket. And he was ready to get down.

My Nehru worked like a magnet. All night long I rocked out with groovy foxes to The Supremes, Deep Purple, The Strawberry Alarm Clock, Steppenwolf, Creedence Clearwater Revival. When The Beatles song *Why Don't We Do It in the Road* blasted through the speakers, every kid with a pulse freaked out, rushing the floor with wild energy, bordering on pandemonium. We couldn't believe the teachers would actually play this song! Didn't they know what the song was about? Who cared!? The song was blaring full blast, so we sang along just as loud:

Why don't we do it in the road?
Why don't we do it in the road?
No one will be watching us,
Why don't we do it in the road?

A couple songs later, I heard the unmistakable organ intro to *Light My Fire*. A roar of recognition rose in the air, as again, kids threw themselves onto the dance floor with abandon. I knew I had to find someone cute to dance with because this tune was about forty-seven minutes long. I made a beeline to a mini-skirted girl named Lisa I'd been eyeballing all night. We hit the dance floor and threw everything we had at the song, waving our arms in the air like we were stricken with seizures, gyrating nonstop until Jim Morrison's final shriek.

Since the dance was nearly over, our teachers decided to mellow the students out after the frenzy of The Doors. So they transitioned quickly to the saccharine sap of *Never My Love* by The Association. Lisa and I weren't quite off the dance floor when we heard the opening strains of the song. Like a knight in shining Nehru, I extended my hand and asked Lisa if she'd like to dance again. If there's one thing a cute chick in a mini skirt can't resist, it's a tall, dark, handsome man with smooth dance moves. Unfortunately, this cute chick had to settle for me.

Never My Love is a slow song. Both of us knew what that meant. It was time to wrap our arms around each other and grope awkwardly. I extended my arms and placed them on Lisa's shoulders. We held onto each other, three feet apart. Gradually, though, we eased into the contours of each other's bodies. Halfway through the song, Lisa laid her head on my left shoulder. Either she had fallen asleep, or she had fallen in love with me. The soaring, melodramatic voices provided the perfect soundtrack for the first flush of young love.

At the end of the song, Lisa and I let go of each other. Then we gazed into each other's eyes. Spontaneously, we drew closer and closer until our lips touched. And then, for what must have been at least two or three seconds, we made out. There, in the storybook setting of a school gymnasium—a mini skirt and a Nehru jacket—sharing a first kiss, in the dreamy dark of an April evening.

* * *

I wish I could say that it was the beginning of a lifelong relationship, that I married my junior high sweetheart, and that we lived happily ever after. The truth is, I never said another word to Lisa. We were too embarrassed to acknowledge that we had kissed, and had no idea what to do or say next. So we avoided each other until the school year ended. That fall, Lisa went to a different high school and I never saw her again. All that's left of that spring evening is a faded snapshot showing a shy, skinny girl in a plaid mini skirt standing beside a goofy teenager who has no idea he looks so nerdy in a Nehru jacket.

SHEAR MADNESS

O VER THE PAST FEW MONTHS there's been a disturbing spate of allegations of sexual misconduct, ranging from groping to child molestation. I'll give you three guesses which gender has been implicated in every allegation. If you said men, you're probably a woman. Either that or you've been paying attention to the litany of charges leveled against powerful men in politics, entertainment, and the media. My wife has long been a firm believer that when it comes to sexual assault, the punishment should fit the crime. Which is why she was so giddy this morning when she read me the story of an Argentine woman who cut off the penis of a man she claims sexually assaulted her. The kicker? She did the deed with a pair of garden shears.

Moments after the story broke, twenty-six year old, Brenda Barattini, was dubbed the Argentinian Lorena Bobbitt. It's been twenty-five years since Lorena "bobbed it." I speak, of course, of the appendage of her abusive husband, John Bobbitt. After enduring years of beatings and rape, Lorena says she snapped, and subsequently snipped, John's manhood with a kitchen knife while he slept. Then she hopped in her car and tossed his junk out the window into a nearby field. Detectives conducted a thorough search of the field, and found Bobbitt's penis (even though it was quite small), so that doctors were able to reattach it. Thereafter, John Bobbitt attained minor celebrity as a porn star, exposing himself to the wider world. Lorena Bobbitt was found not guilty on charges of assault, due to insanity, which caused an "irresistible urge to sexually wound John." She became a hero to women worldwide.

But back to Brenda Barattini. Conflicting stories of the incident have emerged. One version of the story contends that Brenda was in a several month relationship with rock musician, Sergio Fernandez. After discovering messages on Sergio's cell phone that suggested he had been unfaithful to her, she chopped off Sergio's penis and testicles while he slept. If this account is true, all I can say is, the guy must sleep like a rock. Plus, to endure such pain, the dude must have balls of steel. Well,...at least he did.

Another version of the story claims the two were engaged in a sex game in which Sergio was blindfolded. *Hang on a sec, Sergio, while I grab a sex toy.* Then Brenda whips out the gardening shears from a convenient hiding place, and trims Sergio's bush, so to speak. The sex game theory seems the least plausible scenario. I mean, how clueless is this guy that Brenda is able to make three incisions before he catches on that it ain't a game?

Still another version of the story posits that the two knew each other only vaguely. Brenda let Sergio in to the apartment she shared with her brother, because Sergio was an acquaintance of her brother, and had come to retrieve an instrument he had left behind. Being a typical sex-crazed rock musician, he tried to get his rocks off on Brenda. As a lousy musician and a sorry excuse for a man, how was Sergio to know that when he left Brenda's that day he would leave behind a second instrument.

Sergio's lawyer, in an emotional expression of support for her client bemoaned, "It is very possible he's lost the ability to be able to father children." Hallelujah! Please turn your hymnals to "*Oh Happy Day.*"

To assess whether the act was premeditated, investigators are attempting to ascertain where the shears came from. In fact, every woman in Argentina is attempting to ascertain where the shears came from. Because they want a pair. Women throughout South America have suddenly been seized by a keen interest in gardening. Pruning has never been so popular among women. These women are hopeful that what they are about to prune will not grow back any time soon.

Brenda Barattini will undergo a psychiatric evaluation later this month. My guess is that, in light of the insanity of sexual abuse afflicting our world in recent months, Brenda may well be declared one of the sanest women on the planet. She may not have cut out all sexual assaults with a single pair of gardening shears. But at least there's one less dick to worry about.

BACKSEAT DRIVER

W E WERE ON OUR WAY to San Francisco to see the play *Hamilton*. I was riding shotgun in a Tesla driven by Nagesh, who's an executive at the company. The conversation turned to the future of self-driving cars. Nagesh explained that his Tesla had self-driving capabilities. As proof, he removed his hands from the steering wheel, gazed nonchalantly out the driver's side window, and the Tesla made a seamless lane change into the right lane. In the future, he told me, drivers will be able to look at their cell phones or even text while driving. Who would have thought of that? Soon we'll even be able to read a book while we drive. Or stretch out in the back seat of a car.

In the back seat of a car. The very mention of those words dredged up a repressed memory from when I was six years old. In a lightning bolt flash, I remembered that I had been the first person in history to experience a self-driving car. I always was ahead of my time.

It was 1962. My oldest brother, Rob, had just obtained his learner's permit. On the exact day he turned sixteen, he planned to take his driver's test. He couldn't wait until that glorious moment when he would cruise the neighborhood in the family's puke green Rambler and show everybody how cool he was. All he needed was a little practice behind the wheel, and the world was his.

Since this was a major milestone in our family's history, the entire family piled into the Rambler one Saturday afternoon. Mom drove us to the huge empty parking lot behind Valley Fair Shopping Center. She parked miles from any other vehicle, turned off the ignition, and shot my brother a look that said: it's time to get serious. The tension was so thick you could cut it with a rubber spatula. Rob was about to receive his first driving lesson from a master teacher.

Mom flung the car door open, got out, and faced my brother. She instructed him to slide over into the driver's seat. My brother, Dennis, and I, sat in the back seat, filled with nervous excitement, knowing that one day we would be the ones in the driver's seat, learning how to drive one of the ugliest cars ever manufactured in America.

Then came that mind-boggling moment we'd been waiting for. Mom handed Rob the keys, and told him to start the car. With the dexterity of a neurosurgeon, he slid the key into the ignition. Then he twisted the key to the right, simultaneously pressing his foot down on the accelerator, and voila! the engine roared to life. In the backseat, Dennis and I smiled at each other with pride at Rob's superhuman accomplishment. Whoa, we thought, we are related to this genius.

Now, the thing about Mom was, she tended to get a little flustered when she explained things. Because of her fiery Sicilian nature, she was passionate about damn near everything. When she explained something, it came out rapid fire, in a rush of intensity and exuberance. Her mind was always a few steps ahead of her words, so it was natural for her to think she'd already said something, when in fact she hadn't said it at all. The emotional gist of her words was always clear, but she tended to leave out certain key details.

Details like where the brake was and how to use it.

But I'm getting ahead of myself. Right now Rob had successfully started the engine And that '61 Rambler hummed with the mechanical precision of a second-hand lawnmower. Rob sat in the driver's seat, eagerly awaiting further instructions. With the car door still wide open, Mom directed him to release the emergency brake. Then she mimed how to shift the gear selector into Drive. Rob did exactly as he was told. This is where Mom neglecting to tell him about the foot brake became a small matter of concern. Because as soon as Rob shifted into Drive, the car began to move forward. Not fast, but fast enough for someone who had never been behind the wheel of a luxury automobile.

But there was no reason to panic. Dennis and I looked at each other and thought, Hey, this is our older brother. He knows what he's doing. Right. How were we to know the poor slob didn't have a clue?

Meanwhile, Mom is yelling and waving her hands like an apoplectic cheerleader. She's screaming, "The brake! The brake! Push the brake!"

Rob scans the dashboard and starts jabbing at every button he can find. He bangs on the cigarette lighter, activates the windshield wipers, turns on the lights, the defroster. As the car rolls forward at the dizzying speed of five miles an hour, I notice a massive concrete wall looming in the distance that gets closer with every button Rob bashes. But as a six-year-old who has supreme faith in his older brother, I'm still convinced that everything will be fine. And it is. Right up to the moment that Rob jumps out of the car.

Now panic sets in. In spades. Dennis looks at me and I

look at Dennis, and I can see that he's scared out of his wits. And just when I've given up all hope, he does something heroic. He leaps over the front seat and lands in the driver's seat. He places both hands on the steering wheel like a race car driver. And in a moment of single-minded clarity, he thinks, Oh shit! What now? Behind us, Mom is still yelling, "The brake! The brake! Push the brake!"

Dennis searches frantically for the brake. He opens the ashtray, turns on the heater, clicks on the high beams. But he can't find the brake to save his life. Or more importantly, mine. Unlike my oldest brother, though, Dennis has a plan: To get the hell out of there. The door is still wide open. And he'd seen Rob's example only seconds ago. So, following in the footsteps of his role model, Dennis jumps out of the car.

This is the moment where I became the first solo passenger in a self-driving vehicle. I thought it was a lousy idea in 1962, and I think it's an even worse idea today. But did anyone from Tesla ask for my input? Don't get me started!

Sitting there, all alone in the back seat of the Rambler without a seatbelt, I still didn't panic. No, I started bawling my head off. This is it, I thought. I'm gonna die! And it ain't gonna be pretty. When they peel my mangled body off of the concrete wall, the impact will be so staggeringly powerful, I'll be unrecognizable.

Now, I could have been a hero. I could have jumped over the seat and searched for the brake. But even if I did, I couldn't see over the steering wheel, and my feet couldn't reach the pedals. So what was the point? I accepted my fate calmly as I kicked and screamed hysterically. As I did, I forgave my mom for causing my senseless, painful death. Though I wished I could have told her personally not to feel guilty as I gasped my final breaths. That way, she would always remember me with a crippling sense of guilt over the preventable death of her second favorite son. Okay, third.

While I was wallowing in bitterness, Rob (remember him?) had an epiphany. He realized that even though he couldn't drive worth beans, he was a member of his high school track team. After pushing the ejector button in his first driving attempt, he knew the odds of obtaining his driver's license in this lifetime were slim. But the odds of breaking the school's hundred-yard dash record were far more likely. And if there was ever a time for dashing, this was it. A starting gun exploded in his mind, and off he sprinted after the runaway Rambler. Pumping his fists, lifting his knees, getting up on his toes, digging into the parking lot asphalt. In a flash, Rob was right on the tail of the green monster. But time was running faster than both of them. For only fifty feet ahead stood the concrete wall that would be my final resting place.

But a mere concrete wall is no match for a track star. Rob pulled even with the Rambler. And then, like Superman leaping a tall building, he jumped through the open door of the car and into the driver's seat. He pulled his wits about him, and within seconds found the brake pedal. With every ounce of strength he possessed, he slammed on the brake.

The car screeched to a stop. Everything was still and silent. The concrete wall stood unmoving thirty feet away. Rob sat, breathing hard, in the driver's seat. And I was still alive. It was a miracle. I thought, my brother must be Superman: He can't drive for shit, but man can he fly!

* * *

At the time, I credited Rob for saving my life. What a selfless act of bravery. I discovered later his motivation had been my mom threatening he would never drive again if the Rambler ended up with so much as a scratch on it.

Rob eventually learned how to drive, but I believe someone a little less high-strung taught him. He got his license later that year, as did Dennis a few years after that. Me? I waited until I was twenty-seven to learn to drive. I don't think it had anything to do with the runaway car episode. It's just that automobiles seemed like death traps to me. And I've always suspected that concrete walls were out to get me.

So when Nagesh tells me how great the future's going to be with self-driving cars, I don't want to hear it. I've seen that movie before. Next time I'm in a self-driving vehicle that's programmed to drive me straight into a concrete wall, there may not be a track star around to save me.

SPIDER MAN

As a Buddhist I've taken a vow not to kill. Anything. This has proven an easy vow to maintain. Especially when it comes to cute, furry animals. I'm proud to report that I have never killed a single panda, koala, or penguin. Thankfully, I have never encountered these beasts in the wild. They say penguins can be quite ferocious in their natural habitat. My own natural habitat, though, is considerably more dangerous, as it's teeming with swarms of creepy, crawly creatures that would engender homicidal thoughts in even the most committed pacifist. The vast majority of these creatures live within a hundred foot radius of my house. It's my job to save them all. Even the ugly ones.

Take ticks, for instance. Over the past thirty years, I've done a fair amount of running on remote mountain trails that were never intended for human traffic. After one epic trail run in the Sierras, I discovered three ticks attached to my legs. Two of them I plucked off before they could establish permanent residency. But one pesky little sucker was roughly the size of Texas. He had burrowed into the back of my knee and was doing his best Dracula impression. By the end of the run, he'd drunk about half a pint of blood and I was starting to feel lightheaded. I tried desperately to reason with the vampire, but my non-violent pleas fell on deaf ears. Fortunately, I recalled that if you light a match, the tick will leave peacefully. And I have to say, he did. Other than the third-degree burns I sustained from lighting the back of my knee on fire, this method worked quite effectively. Thanks to my benevolence, that tick will live long enough to infect another dozen people with Lyme disease.

Don't even get me started on cockroaches. Donde esta la cucaracha? In my classroom. Es verdad! For ten years I taught in a classroom that was infested with these prehistoric vermin. At odd moments, they would emerge from the walls and gross out my middle school students. *Surprise!* I would tell my hormonally challenged students to remain calm. That I was trained at cockroach search and rescue. Always eager to help, my students would volunteer to squash the disgusting things with their Converse sneakers. But I would take the high road and patiently inform them that no living thing would die in my classroom. Yes, I would explain, with utmost compassion, that if any little acne-pocked punk killed a cockroach, he was dead meat. Cowering in their chairs, my students would watch wide-eyed while I fetched my Cockroach Catcher: a mini Dixie cup and a 3 x 5 index card. With dead aim, I would swoop down with the Dixie cup, temporarily imprisoning the roach, and then deftly slide the index card underneath. Then, with the speed of The Flash, I would sprint to the door and deposit the cockroach in the dirt outside the classroom. In this heroic fashion, I managed to save whole generations of cockroaches. Or, it could have been the same roach coming back five hundred times.

In my next life, I'm certain I'll be reincarnated as Spider Man, as the result of the good karma I've accrued from saving hundreds of spiders. I can't tell you how many mornings I've stumbled into the bathroom, wanting only to press the porcelain, when I find myself eye to compound eye with a humongous, hairy spider. Mindful of my vow, I rush to the kitchen in search of my Spider Scooper (a variation on the Cockroach Catcher, only with a real glass instead of a Dixie cup). Careful not to injure any of its eight legs, I capture the squirming arachnid in my cruelty-free trap and dash to the front door.

With the strength of The Hulk, I throw the door open, exposing my Fruit of the Looms to the traumatized neighbors. I squat down, remove the index card, shake the spider out of the glass, and run like hell. Even though I'm a veteran runner, I'm no match for an octoped. I slam the door shut and deadbolt it. But I know, in a matter of minutes, there'll be a faint knocking on the door. Yeah, I don't like to admit it, but some of them will be back. I've abolished the death penalty in our house, but there's a high recidivism rate. What can I say? I do my best. My job is to liberate spiders. Someone else will have to rehabilitate them.

I can hear you thinking, what an incredible sacrifice this guy is making for the benefit of sentient beings. Well, someone has to take a stand for these poor, helpless creatures whose only defenses are razor-sharp fangs, a deadly venom and a lust for blood. So I'm sticking to my vow never to kill insects. I just hope they don't kill me first.

WE'LL ALWAYS
HAVE MACY'S

W HEN I WAS A MERE lad of twenty-two, I had a dream job. I paid my way through college by directing plays at elementary schools through the local parks and recreation department. As a young theatre student, I considered myself a working theatre professional. Not only was the pay decent, the hours fit into my schedule at the University perfectly, and I was given the freedom to write and produce my own plays. Ah, life was good.

But then tragedy struck. Anti-tax crusader, Howard Jarvis, believed that big government entitlements, epitomized by socialistic fluff such as after-school theatre programs, were burying citizens beneath an avalanche of ever-escalating property taxes. Jarvis devised a plan to amend the California Constitution to restructure property taxes so that individuals who had owned their homes for many years would pay lower taxes than newer or first time home buyers. The result of his campaign to curtail runaway government spending was a referendum called Proposition 13. It passed overwhelmingly at the polls in the summer of 1978, which led almost instantly to a slashing of social services at the local level. One of the first things cut—you guessed it—was my job directing plays with the parks and recreation.

I read about the passage of Prop. 13 in the *New York Times* in Manhattan, where I was performing for a month. The eternally optimistic and perpetually naive members of our theatre collective consoled me. Hey, it probably won't be that bad, they commiserated. The State of California wouldn't be so heartless as to cut such an important program. Maybe something good will come out of it.

Armed with their infectious enthusiasm, I returned to California, ready to get back to work. The day I got back, I called my supervisor, asking her if Prop. 13 had affected my job status. There was a long pause, followed by an apologetic explanation that my dream job had been eliminated.

Now, you would think that my landlord, who had just realized a huge reduction in his property taxes, would have been sympathetic to my plight. But apparently he still wanted his rent. On time. The beginning of the month was rapidly approaching and I was a few bucks shy of covering the rent, not to mention food and utilities. I needed the immediacy of a quick paycheck. So I grabbed a dogeared phonebook and looked up the number for Kelly Services.

At the time, Kelly Services was the premier temporary employment agency, finding work for the unemployed or those who were in professional transition. Until very recently, Kelly Services had been called Kelly Girls, and was primarily a pool of professional women with clerical and secretarial skills. Somewhere along the line— probably as the result of a gender discrimination lawsuit—the agency was renamed Kelly Services, a change that reflected inclusion of both genders in their hiring policies. That way, a persecuted white male, whose only marketable skill was the ability to emote, would no longer be the target of discrimination.

The next morning I reported to Kelly Services' central office. I completed an application which detailed my skills and interests. Since I had none, other than an obsession with avant-garde theater and 1960s rock music, it was assessed that I would be best suited as a retail inventory lackey. It wasn't Shakespeare, but at least I had a title. I was told to report the following Monday morning to Macy's.

That was the day I would begin my true dream job: stocking shelves in Macy's lingerie department. Kelly Services must have known intuitively that I was an expert in the field of ladies' intimate apparel, skills I had honed through years of extensive research in scholarly periodicals such as *Playboy* and *Penthouse*. It was the culmination of a lifetime of study.

Upon my arrival on that auspicious morning, I was introduced to my supervisor, Mrs. Elaine Bradford. Mrs. Bradford was a buxom, domineering woman with an air of confidence. A consummate professional, it didn't take long for me to realize, this was a woman who knew her way around a pair of panties.

After an exchange of pleasantries, Mrs. Bradford explained in her sultry voice that lingerie was a highly specialized field that demanded the utmost attention to detail. She stated in no uncertain terms, that in our professional relationship she would expect nothing less than unwavering obedience to her commands. Oh, behave!

And then, with a sensuous gesture, she explained that my first task would be to hang the pile of brassieres on the table to her left onto a nearby rack.

I can say, without reservation, that I have never taken to a task so willingly, or worked with such relish. The Simon and Garfunkel song with the "feelin' groovy" refrain kept looping through my mind while I worked:

Slow down, you're moving too fast,
You've got to make the morning last.

I labored to suppress a grin, for fear someone would catch my eye and think I was some kind of pervert. Thanks to my theatrical training, I maintained an almost clinical expression. But inside, I was grinning like a court jester who just pulled a prank on the king.

Over the course of that week, I became the model employee, completing every task Mrs. Bradford laid before me with delight. It dawned on me that this could develop into a career path for me if I played my cards right. And from her suggestive comments, and the palpable tension developing between Mrs. Bradford and me, I had the unmistakable impression that I was playing my cards just right.

By Wednesday, I had become Mrs. Bradford's most trusted employee. She rewarded my slavish devotion by promoting me to camisoles and then to bustiers. On Thursday, I was handling teddies and corsets. By Friday, I had graduated to garter belts.

That weekend was achingly long. My sleep was fitful, filled with lurid dreams of Elaine Bradford, longing for the coming Monday morning when I would gaze into her penetrating eyes and inquire, "What can I do for you today, Mrs. Bradford?"

That long awaited Monday reunion never came. For upon reporting to work after that interminable weekend, Mrs. Elaine Bradford was nowhere to be found. I searched high and low for a glimpse of her zaftig form, sniffing the air for a hint of her intoxicating fragrance. My heart, as well as my nostrils, were left unrequited.

As I fumbled halfheartedly, sorting a pile of fishnet stockings, I received the earth-shattering news that Mrs. Bradford had accepted a lucrative position as manager of a recently opened branch of Frederick's of Hollywood, and would not be returning to Macy's.

She never even said goodbye.

Without Mrs. Bradford there to groom me, things just weren't the same. Later that day, a severe, German woman named Hilda replaced Mrs. Bradford. As the pet employee of the previous supervisor, I knew my days were numbered. Sure enough, Hilda insisted on a fresh start in ladies intimates and decided to clean house.

At the end of the day, I was laid off. It was humiliating. They gave me a pink slip. And it wasn't even my size.

FOULED UP

G ROWING UP IN THE BAY Area during the heyday of the San Francisco Giants, I had a dream. It wasn't what you're thinking—that one day I'd become the next Willie Mays or Juan Marichal. No, my dream was far simpler and much more attainable. I dreamed that one day, while sitting in the stands along the third base line on a lazy summer afternoon, I would catch a foul ball.

Countless summer afternoons I spent with my Uncle Johnny sitting in the grandstands at Candlestick Park. To every game, I brought my well-worn glove, in hopes of snagging a foul tip. And I came so close, so many times. If only my arm had been about a hundred and fifty feet longer, I'd have a box full of souvenir baseballs. But since the game ain't horseshoes, regrettably, I never caught that elusive foul ball of my dreams.

But one night, when I was about forty, I had a vivid dream in which I was sitting in the stands at our local minor league stadium and caught a foul ball. I saw a vision of myself holding the ball up in triumph, while the crowd cheered. I awoke the next morning, a man with a mission. My date with destiny could not be postponed. I dug out my pocket schedule for the San Jose Giants. And behold! They were playing in town on that very afternoon. I proposed the idea of going to the ballpark to my wife, Wren, omitting the part about my dream, for fear she would have me

39

institutionalized. I lapsed into sweet talk mode, telling Wren I had a great idea. I was going to take her out to the ball game.

Yippie!

On Wren's scale of enjoyable ways to spend an afternoon, going to a ball game registers just below defrosting the refrigerator and scrubbing the toilet. But being a supportive wife, increasingly aware of her husband's mid-life crisis, she agreed. I think she felt she owed a certain debt to baseball players, whose mere image in the mind's eye of her husband had prolonged intimate physical exertions on numerous occasions. As much as she hated the sport, Wren had to admit: Baseball been berry berry good to her.

The next thing we knew, we found ourselves inside the 4,200-seat capacity, Municipal Stadium. I'd been to Muni at least fifty times before and had studied trajectory, prevailing winds, solar positioning and aisle access, so that I was able to select prime seats in foul ball territory. We sat in a section just below the press box that we had virtually to ourselves. That way, when a foul ball cracked off a bat in our direction, I wouldn't have to push a little old lady down to catch it. It would be all mine, baby! Because today, just like in my dream, I was going to catch a foul ball.

By the third inning, the sun rose to its zenith. The section where we sat was mercilessly exposed to the sun. That's when I remembered that not only is Wren fair-haired and fair-skinned, she wasn't wearing a hat and is highly susceptible to melanoma. Always the sensitive individual, I reflected, Perhaps a cool drink and some light snacks might help.

"Hey, sweetie, how about a lemonade and a bag of peanuts?"

"Okay. Thanks." Wren said, containing her enthusiasm,

so that I wouldn't think she enjoyed baseball games and drag her back next weekend.

As I walked down the concourse to the concession stand, I thought to myself, Wren's really enjoying this. What a great time we're having together. Just wait till I get back. I'm gonna teach her how to throw peanut shells on the ground and spill her lemonade. Hell, I might even teach her how to belch. Man, this will be a day she'll never forget.

But when I returned, I could see Wren was in a state of agitation.

"What's wrong?" I asked, handing her the iced lemonade.

"Something really scary just happened!"

"What's that?"

"Just after you left, a ball came straight at me."

"What did you do?"

"What do you think I did? I jumped out of the way!"

"You didn't try to catch the ball?"

"Of course not! Why would I do that?"

"If you catch the ball, you get to keep it."

"I don't want a damned baseball! I was worried about getting a concussion. That thing was coming at me a hundred miles an hour."

"Well, what happened to the ball?"

"It hit right there where you were sitting. It bounced off your seat and some little old lady ended up with it."

Say it ain't so, Joe! I waited for years to catch that ball. I followed the instructions of the baseball gods to a tee, from the prophetic dream to finding the exact right seat. But thanks to a lousy lemonade and a bag of stale peanuts, my dream got fouled up. Once again, the mighty Casey had struck out.

Still, I know somewhere out there is a foul ball with my name on it. Next time, I'll be ready. But I don't want to get prematurely excited about it. So until then, all I can do is think of baseball players.

MEXICAN STANDOFF

I'VE NEVER THOUGHT OF MYSELF as cruise material. Don't get me wrong. I like free food and drinks and tropical breezes as much as the next guy. But the thought of being surrounded by a peer group of balding lushes whose idea of a vacation is having access to processed food twenty-four hours a day, and scarfing three desserts with every meal, holds about as much interest to me as a week in Mar-a-Lago. But when my old pal, Bob, offered me a ticket to a world-class music cruise after his son cancelled, I figured, what the hell. For a week, I'll be cruise material.

Wren begged me not to go. She has this irrational fear that I'll fall off the boat as I navigate a tight turn around the jogging deck and end up as shark bait. She's fond of the movie, *Titanic*, and she's certain the ship will collide with a massive iceberg, and that my body won't be recovered for a hundred years. I explain to her that we're sailing to the Caribbean where there are no icebergs. She rolls her eyes and scoffs, "That's what the passengers on the Titanic thought. Right before they plunged to their deaths!"

If the icebergs don't get me, she's convinced pirates will overpower the ship, gouge out my eye, chop off my leg, and force me to slur my speech like Keith Richards. If I manage to escape with my life, she worries I'll return with an eye patch, a wooden leg, and a creepy attraction to parrots. I attempt to reassure her with evidence from the

43

internet that proves that the vast majority of pirate attacks occur off the coast of Somalia. "Yeah," she sneers. "That must be why they call it *Pirates of Somalia*, instead of *Pirates of the Caribbean*."

"If you insist on going on this stupid boat trip," she rants, "at least promise me you won't get off the boat in Mexico." She fears I'll be kidnapped by a violent drug cartel and forced to sneak across the border as a drug mule, only to be deported back to Mexico, and separated from my college-aged daughter, who was brought here as a child, and is only trying to pursue her dream.

I tell Wren to relax. The last thing Mexicans want to do is have contact with Americans. They may be criminals and rapists and drug dealers, but they're not dumb.

But now Bob and I are standing at the edge of a dead-end road in Mexico, and Wren's darkest fears are about to be realized. We were driven here at ninety miles an hour, by an unlicensed taxi driver, named El Chapo. As he drove, he grinned at us in his rear view mirror, careening from the shoulder of the road to the center divide, taking us from the safety of downtown Cozumel to this dead-end road where the trackless jungle begins.

When the car screeches to a stop, the driver says, "This is as far as I can take you."

Before you kill us? a voice inside my head whispers.

As we stumble out of the car, Bob glances to his right and notices a godforsaken trail extending into the jungle. The trail leads to the site of the mass graves of the dipshit runners who've come before us. Tangled in the branches of a dead tree nearby are the tattered remnants of a decomposing Nike t-shirt.

"This trail," Bob inquires of the taxi driver, "is it safe?"

Of course it's not safe! There are bandidos in the bushes

and outlaws in the trees. Deadly vipers are lurking in the undergrowth, ready to squeeze the life out of us, and devour us whole. Hell no, it's not safe.

"Yes, it's safe," the driver replies, "But there are a lot of potholes."

Did you hear that, Bob? Potholes! These are not the harmless American variety of pothole seen on our city streets, where if you hit one, all you have to do is spend three thousand dollars for a new front-end alignment. You stumble into one of these bad boys, you can kiss your ass goodbye.

Just as I'm about to inform Bob that I've decided to ride back into town with the driver, his sanity is restored, and he turns his attention away from the potholed trail to the pull of the cool, blue Caribbean in the distance. The driver speeds off in a cloud of exhaust, and we begin the long, slow jog back to town.

Forty minutes later, our run completed, we're walking down a backstreet in search of a lesser touristed shopping district. There are pharmacies on every block that sell everything from Prozac to testosterone — at a fraction of the price you'd pay at home, Bob explains. They don't need no stinkin' FDA in Mey-hee-co. Pay your money, put the shit in a plastic bag, and be done with it.

Oddly enough, Bob seems to know these pharmacies intimately. That's when it hits me that the real purpose of his annual cruise is right here on these backstreets. He doesn't give a damn about the music; he's here to stock up on his yearly supply of Viagra. No wonder he's taking an online course in Spanish. So he can order his erectile dysfunction meds like a local: "Hola, Señor. Muchos Viagra, por favor. ¿Donde esta la biblioteca?"

While I'm having my revelation, Bob's eye is drawn to

a small corner farmacia. He tells me he's got to slip in there for a moment and why don't I wander up the block and see if there's any tacky tourist crap I want to buy. He speaks in the hushed tones of the hustler, from Stevie Wonder's *Living For The City,* who cons a hayseed into running drugs across a street in New York City.

Before I can say vaya con Dios, Bob has vanished into Pancho's Farmacia, and I find myself wandering into increasingly less populated and more hostile territory. Half a block up, I notice three men sitting on folding chairs in front of a small shop. They appear to be convicts who escaped from a maximum security prison that morning. They eyeball me like a tamale they are intent on devouring. I'm fresh carne to these bad hombres.

One of them calls me pendejo, which I believe is a term of endearment. I throw up my left hand in a lame greeting, trying to maintain my cool. I want these desperadoes to know that I'm not the ugly American. Though I am ugly. And an American. I want them to understand I'm not a tourist. I'm just a regular guy who got off a cruise ship and decided to take a tour. Of the touristy part of this tourist town. As part of my tour.

Two of the three amigos glare at me, transmitting veiled threats of violence with their scowls. The third jumps up and shoves a cigar box under my nose.

"You like to smoke ceegars?"

"No gracias," I reply, in the weakest Spanish accent he'll hear all day.

"Come into my shop. I'll sell you whatever you like to smoke."

Yeah, right. Do I look like I have loco stamped on my forehead? I explain to him in Gringlish that I don't smoke anything, that I'm just trying to kill time while my friend, who just ditched me, buys a thousand Viagra tablets at a third the price he can buy them for in the States. Something's lost in translation, though, because he continues to lure me in to his shop with a litany of exotic strains of Mexican marijuana: Oaxacan...Michoacán...Acapulco Gold...

I pretend to be interested in some bric-a-brac hanging in a shop across the way. I veer sharply to my right, while Potzo Villa drones on with his sales pitch. I turn in a wide arc, swing a hundred and eighty degrees around, then break into a sprint back to the farmacia. Thank God I'm wearing my running shoes, or I would never have been able to outrun these homicidal potheads. I reach the farmacia, winded, just as Bob glides out of the doorway with a sheepish grin. And no wonder. He's a new man. Or at least he will be when the drugs kick in.

"A guy tried to sell me weed back there, Bob."

Bob calms me down in the worldly wise tone of a seasoned traveller. "Nine times out of ten, guys like that are narcs. They sell you a nickel bag for a few pesos, next thing you know you're shacked up with a pederast in some sleazy prison. You pay 'em a couple hundred US dollars and you're a free gringo."

How does Bob know all this? Wait a minute! The full picture is starting to come into sharp focus. Bob knows these streets like the back of his hand...He owns property in Honduras...He likes Mexican food! That whole thing back there was a set-up. Bob's in cahoots with these bad hombres!

"Señor, you send your amigo estupido up the street so we can rob him. You hide en la farmacia and pretend to buy Viagra. We'll get him to buy some marijuana in the back of Miguel's tienda. Since he's an old hippie on vacacion, with mucho dinero, he'll probably buy a kilo. When he does, we show him our stinkin' badges and vamonos to la prisión. If he pays us three hundred dólares, we say it was all a beeg misunderstanding and let him go. For your help, we pay you one hundred pesos and give you a year's supply of your prescripción of choice. ¿Comprendes?"

"Si, Señor," Bob agrees, with an impeccable Spanish accent. And just like that, forty years of friendship are flushed down the toilet.

How could I be so stupid? I should have listened to Wren. Turns out her fears were perfectly rational. In the future, she can prevent me from crossing the border by building a wall between the US and Mexico. The only question is who's going to pay for it.

SLEEPLESS IN SNORESVILLE

WHEN I WAS A CHILD, I spake as a child, I understood as a child, I thought as a child. But when I became an old fart, I put away childish things and began to snore and grow nose hair like other geezers my age. The nose hair's not a problem. My hairstylist says if I grow it out, she can braid it into pigtails. Then I can tie the pigtails together and hang beads from them.

The snoring, on the other hand, has become something of an issue. Not for me. For my wife, Wren. She insists that I'm doing it on an increasingly regular basis, and that I'm doing it intentionally, just to piss her off.

Since I've never actually heard myself snore, I have to take it on faith from Wren, who's threatening to record me. That way, not only will she have proof of my snoring, she'll be able to play it for me full blast in the middle of the night, so that she won't be the only one kept awake. And on those rare occasions when I'm away from home, she can listen to my prerecorded snoring and recall how lovely it would have been to have me beside her, so she could give me a sharp jab in the ribs and tell me to shut up.

At the root of the snoring problem is the fact that Wren has hypersensitive hearing. Though, *selective* hypersensitive hearing might be more accurate. She can't hear me talk in

49

crowded restaurants, but she hears pitches even dogs can't hear. If the sound is annoying, Wren hears it crystal clear — babies crying, planes flying over our house, millennials talking on cell phones who use "like" in every sentence. A few years ago, she made me aware of a family of raccoons that pad across our roof at night. Thanks to her sensitive hearing, I now lay awake nights, anticipating a raccoon invasion that, as an animal lover and pacifist, I will be unable to defend against. With a pack of rabid raccoons squatting in our spare bedroom, snoring will be the least of Wren's worries.

To complicate things further, Wren has developed into something of an insomniac. Due to her acute auditory perception, she stares at the ceiling most nights, tuning in to every sound frequency above ten decibels. Her hearing is so attuned that the sound of a model husband's normal breathing pattern sounds to her like the roar of an angry lion. Now she's beginning to think like an angry lion. Having lain awake countless nights, she's had ample opportunity to contemplate the efficacy of using her pillow to suffocate me. Sure, Wren's aware that the pillow strategy will place her in a real life episode of *Orange Is the New Black*, but at least it will solve the problem.

To her credit, before she resorts to drastic measures, Wren's willing to explore less violent options. She's convinced that I snore because I sleep on my back. She explains through clenched teeth that people who sleep on their sides don't snore. I tell her she has no proof of that.

"Oh really?" she fumes. She grabs her laptop like a weapon, and flips it open to conduct a vindictive Google search. Jabbing the keys violently, she types in, Do people snore when they sleep on their backs?

"Look at that;" she gushes, "it's the first thing that pops

up!" as if it's the most frequently asked internet question. She verifies her theory by citing the anecdotal research of a fringe website, maintained by a woman on death row who claims that even though her husband still sleeps on his back, he no longer snores in his coffin.

Wren throws up her hands at my unwillingness to sleep on my side, even though I tell her it could lead to chronic sciatica.

"So what?" she sneers. "It might give you a pain in the ass, but at least you wouldn't **be** a pain in the ass!"

"Thank God for earplugs!" she says one night, with a sense of resignation. She switches off the bedside light, and turns away from me, wearing sleek, pink earplugs that prevent her from hearing airplanes, raccoons and snoring husbands. How did it come to this? We used to be little lovebirds who thought every idiosyncrasy was adorable, and only added to the other person's irresistible charm.

Now that the lights are out, I stare at the ceiling, brainstorming ways to rekindle our romance. Perhaps I can begin by removing those pink earplugs and whispering sweet nothings in her ear. There's no telling what that could lead to. It might keep us both awake, but I'm pretty sure it will prevent me from snoring.

STARVING CHILDREN IN CHINA

I T WAS BEATEN INTO MY thick skull as a kid that I should eat everything on my plate. Having survived the Great Depression, my mom learned the hard way that food should never go to waste. And she reminded me about five times a day.

At the dinner table, when I pretended to be repulsed by the slimy spinach wiggling on my plate, Mom laid the classic guilt trip on me: "There are starving children in China who would love to eat that spinach."

It was always China, where I imagined half the population was dying of starvation. According to Mom, there was zero food in China. That's why we fought to keep the Iron Curtain in place. Otherwise, those Commies would come and steal all our food. And love every bite.

Which would have been fine with me. Every time Mom started droning on about starving kids in China, I prayed some emaciated Chinese kid would magically appear in our dining room. *Finally! You want my spinach? Help yourself! How 'bout this liver? You like Brussels sprouts? Knock yourself out, pal.* I would have gladly done my part to end world hunger. But I suspected that, despite what Mom said, Chinese kids hated spinach just as much as I did. Starving kids aren't stupid.

Now, I appreciate the message my mom was trying to impart. In retrospect, I realize she was right. As an immigrant child, never more than a step away from being a starving kid herself, food waste was sacrilegious to her. Further, she wanted to ensure that I was healthy by feeding me nutritious meals from the four food groups. But I was looking out for number one. I couldn't care less if the food was good for me. Just as long as it tasted good. My own nutritional plan was based primarily on two major food groups: dessert and candy.

Fed up one evening over my refusal to eat some mystery vegetable, Mom exploded. "One day all you're getting for dinner is a big bowl of candy!"

How I prayed for the day she would make good on that threat. Then, for once, I could have guaranteed that I would clean my plate and ask for seconds. Sadly, my repast of candy never materialized.

To ensure we ate plenty of vegetables, Mom used to make Italian-style zucchini with olive oil, oregano and garlic. Yuck! I hated it. It was oily and mushy and tasteless. Yet, it was on our plates at least once a week. I tried my best to hide the zucchini beneath my spaghetti, to spread it around the plate, to smash it into pulp, to stash it in my napkin. All to no avail. Mom was wise to all of my tricks and would force me to eat all of it before she served dessert. She insisted there were starving children in Italy who would love to eat my zucchini.

One night a couple years before I was born, my brother, Dennis, wouldn't eat his zucchini. My dad looked at him puzzled, "You don't like zucchini pie?"

My brother, who didn't develop common sense until his adult years, took the bait. "This is pie?"

My dad laid it on thick, like an actor in a soap opera.

"Yes, that's zucchini pie." Needless to say, my brother devoured every slimy bite of his zucchini that night. He was thirty-five before he realized that if it doesn't have a crust, it ain't pie.

Through the years, I've found that some lessons I tried so hard to resist have sunk in with a vengeance. As our resident chef (I speak euphemistically, as labeling me a chef is laughably pretentious), I try to make just the right amount of food that Wren and I will consume in an evening with no leftovers. Every night we attempt to eat everything on our plates, to be members of the Clean Plate Club. Pretty pathetic, I know. But no other clubs will have us as members.

I love salad. So at the beginning of each week, I whip out the old salad spinner and mix up a big batch of lettuce that I use for salads through the week. I store the lettuce in a Pyrex container that lives in the refrigerator. One week not long ago, for some reason, we weren't eating many salads, and the lettuce remained in the container for almost two weeks. At the end of the second week, not wanting to waste perfectly good lettuce, I opened the container. Lifting the lid, I was assaulted by the overpowering whiff of decay. But the lettuce was still green, which I believe was its original color. And it looked edible—mostly. Besides, this was organic, artisanal romaine lettuce, and I couldn't very well throw it away. I knew there were starving children in the affluent backstreets of Saratoga who would love to eat my artisanal lettuce.

So I tossed it all into a bowl and mixed it with some chopped vegetables. I had learned my childhood lesson well. Never waste food, even when it smells suspicious. I asked Wren if she would like a bowl. But seeing that there was only enough lettuce for one salad, she insisted, with her customary generosity, that I eat the whole thing. Little did I know, her actions were not entirely altruistic.

The next morning I bounded out of bed. As I was slipping on my socks, I felt woozy, and had to grab hold of the dresser to steady my balance. I didn't think much of it until I was doing my yoga. After only a few minutes, I knew something was seriously wrong. The room started spinning and wouldn't stop. I felt like I was on one of those playground merry-go-rounds; and my stomach churned like I had just stepped off of one. My head throbbed. I was feverish. I broke out in a sweat. I had a metallic taste in my mouth. Almost an hour passed before the constant circular motion ceased. I spent the day as if recuperating from a hangover.

I found out that food poisoning is quite common with romaine lettuce. The thick leaves are the ideal breeding ground for a fungal infection called Sclerotinia. Bacteria, including E. coli and salmonella, hides inside the folds of the leaves, ready to poison schmucks like me who don't believe in wasting food. My God! All I wanted to do was be resourceful. No, I don't want to contribute to the growth of landfills, but is food waste the hill I want to die on? From now on, when I smell decomposed vegetable matter or see discolored leaves in my salad, I'm throwing it out! Sure, there may be starving children in Africa who would love to eat my salad, but they'd be better off with a bowl of candy. At least it won't poison them.

OUR LADY OF THE HOLY CHEETO

A COUPLE MONTHS AGO, A MAN in San Antonio, Texas claims he had a religious encounter when he beheld a Cheeto that bore a striking resemblance to the Virgin Mary. I know what you're thinking. A Cheeto? Seriously? The cynics among us may scoff at the Texan's experience, as well as his taste in snack foods, but the seer from San Antone is not alone.

In 2004, a Florida woman glimpsed the visage of the Virgin Mary in a toasted cheese sandwich. Upon seeing the vision of Our Lady, the woman reputedly stashed the sandwich away in a top secret hiding place. When she pulled it out ten years later, she found, miraculously, that the sandwich was perfectly preserved, with nary a sign of mold or decay. In a selfless act of religious piety, she auctioned the sandwich on eBay for $71, a sum she declared was "heaven sent," as it was the exact amount she needed to pay that month's rent on her double wide trailer.

Divine apparitions such as these are not limited to the Madonna (even though she popularized the song *Like a Virgin*). In 2015, in Oaxaca, Mexico, Enedina Mendoza was preparing homemade tortillas in her humble kitchen. One tortilla among many proved to be particularly problematic, as it refused to brown, no matter how much heat Enedina applied to it. So she inspected the tortilla up close and personal, and lo, she gazed upon the holy face of Jesus staring at her from the depths of the corn tortilla. This was all the proof Enedina needed to renew her faith, knowing that Jesus was watching her every move.

In 1996, in Nashville, Tennessee, baristas at Bongo Java Coffee discovered the image of Mother Teresa in a cinnamon bun. Reverently nicknamed the "Nun Bun" by the Bongo staff, it was proudly displayed as a holy relic. Tragically, though, the bun was stolen during a 2005 break-in at the coffee house, along with $300 in cash, which the thieves purportedly used to erect a sacred shrine to the Nun Bun in their meth lab.

Over the years, these supernatural visions have increased exponentially, as one adherent claims to have seen the image of Jesus in a Kit Kat Bar. Another maintains he saw Jesus in a Lay's Sour Cream and Onion potato chip. A believer in West Virginia, while searching under the seat of his car, swears he saw Mary *and* Jesus in a Funyun. Not to be outdone, a devout Christian saw the Virgin Mary and the baby Jesus in a pretzel.

By analyzing the testimonies of the chosen few, two patterns tend to emerge. With the exception of the tortilla maker, all of these visionaries tend to be fond of junk food. Likely, this contributes to their second sightedness. And, I may be going out on a limb here, but I'm guessing most of them smoke crack.

But then, who am I to cast aspersions on these chosen ones? It's easy for me to deride these mystics when I've never experienced the paranormal. Perhaps instead of adhering to a nutritionally balanced diet that's low in sodium and high in fiber, I should be consuming more

Funyuns and Cheetos. Then, maybe I would be more receptive to mystical episodes.

And even if these people are completely whacked out of their minds, as I suspect they are, maybe they're on to something. It's not like they're hurting anyone. They're seeing what they want to see: benevolent, loving images of revered holy figures. They've cultivated a second sight that transforms the mundane into the sacred. We should all be so deluded.

What if all these years I've been searching for the divine in all the wrong places, when it's been right in front of me,... on aisle eight, right next to the Nacho Cheese Flavored Doritos. I always hoped that one day I would see God. I just never expected it to be in a Pop Tart.

BATTERED AND BLOODIED

I KNOW I RUN THE RISK of sounding like an insufferable old crank when I say this. But kids today are a bunch of wusses. There, I said it.

Back when I was a kid, I breathed toxic pollution, drank contaminated water, rode in cars without seatbelts or safety features. The walls of my house oozed asbestos and exposed lead paint. The apples I ate to keep the doctor away were laced with DDT. I fortified my body twelve ways with Wonder Bread and TV dinners and Twinkies and maraschino cherries soaked in Red Dye Number 2. And I'm still alive to talk about it.

Bicycle helmets? Yeah, I wore one. I called it a baseball hat. I slammed my head on concrete so many times, I had asphalt dust on my shoulders instead of dandruff. You think that stopped me? Shoot, if I fell, I shook it off, adjusted my blurred vision and kept pedaling until I ran into the next tree or parked car. Sure, I might have sustained a few brain traumas. But look how I turned out.

Recently, I conducted a scientific analysis of my near-death encounters as a kid and concluded that my life expectancy should have been somewhere between nine or ten years. Should have been. But did I take the last train to Curtainsville? No, I defied the odds. You know why? Cause I'm not a weenie.

If you're one of these lily-livered lollipops born after the

61

50s and 60s, you have no idea what it was like. Childhood was fraught with peril in those days. Take playgrounds, for instance. They were designed to inflict injury.

We played on jungle gyms and monkey bars made of metal pipe strong enough to withstand an atomic blast. When you fell from the top of one — which I did every day of my childhood, you landed on hard packed dirt that had less give than concrete. If you ended up with only a broken bone or two, you picked yourself up, wiped off the dirt, and climbed back on for more abuse. You've seen those swings at parks with those soft plastic seats to prevent injury? Those are for sissies. Swings in my day were created for kids with square butts who were fond of wedgies. At our school playground, the swings were made of un-sanded wood. By the time I was seven, I had so many splinters in my ass, I looked like a pin cushion. But it was nothing a pair of industrial strength tweezers couldn't fix.

These gutless wonders today should be grateful they're living in an era when the most serious menace is gluten intolerance. Back in the day, there were psychopaths running loose. And most of them lived in my neighborhood.

Once, when I was about three years old, I snuck outside and down the block to see Sandra, a five-year-old I had the hots for. Today, if I wandered three houses away from home by myself, I'd be kidnapped and sold on the black market to a survivalist couple in Wichita. But since I was born a ramblin' man, I navigated my way to Sandra's corner house no problem. Then I told her I wanted to get a play date started up in here.

Now, Sandra was the love of my life. There was just one slight problem with our relationship. Sandra hated my guts. In a pattern that was to recur throughout my life, she let me know that she was a classy dame, that I wasn't in her league. And then, with impeccable manners, she told me to get lost before she smacked me one.

Well, even at the age of three, I knew when a lady was playing hard to get. So I took it to the next level. I got the party started all by myself, running around Sandra's yard like the carefree little devil I was then and still am. When I wouldn't scram, Sandra's voice took on an edge. She told me that she didn't play with babies, and if I didn't make like a bakery truck and haul buns, she would resort to drastic measures. Oblivious to the danger this older woman posed to my safety, I continued dancing around like a demented dervish.

Frustrated by my immature antics, Sandra decided there was only one way to get rid of a pest like me. She picked up a piece of aluminum tubing, left over from the recently erected tetherball pole in her front yard, raised it up, and whacked me upside the head.

Do you think I bawled like a little crybaby and ran home to my mommy? You're darn right I did! And Sandra ran right behind me, thinking she'd killed me. She prayed she wouldn't have to spend the rest of her life locked up in Alcatraz for attempted homicide.

By the time I reached home, the knot on my skull swelled to the size of Half Dome. I threw myself into my mom's dress, knowing she would get a restraining order, sue Sandra's parents, and punch the little brat's lights out. Yeah, I wish. Mom perused the knot on my head nonchalantly and said, "You'll be fine." Then she stuck a Band-Aid on my head, patted me on the back, and sent me back outside to play tetherball. We never even went to see a doctor. If I'd had an MRI and years of rehabilitation, I could have attended an Ivy League school—especially if my IQ had been higher than my body temperature, and I turned in my homework every now and then. I could have been a lawyer or a CEO and made millions of dollars. But I took my lumps and made the most of my diminished brain capacity. That's the way we rolled back in the day.

I'm lucky I still have all my toes and fingers. One time I was in my backyard, sawing a tiny piece of wood that I balanced off the edge of a chair with my left hand. Something overhead — probably a squirrel on the fence — caught my attention. Being an expert at multi-tasking, I glanced up for a better look. As I did, the rusty saw blade sliced in to my left thumb, straight to the bone. Blood began spurting up like something out of a Monty Python sketch. I screamed bloody murder and rushed in to the house, a trail of red blotches behind me. My mom saw my panic and my pain, and did what any caring mother in the 1960s would have done. She poured half a bottle of iodine on the wound.

My blood curdling scream shattered our next door neighbor's fine china. Could mollycoddled kids today do that? Hell no. They're taught to use their inside voices. There was no such thing as inside voices in the 60s. I screamed, hoping to get sympathy from my mom. Nice try. Mom told me to suck it up, that I was making a huge deal over a few pints of blood and a little iodine. Then she wrapped a Band-Aid around my thumb, patted me on the back, and sent me outside to saw more wood. No stitches, no emergency room visit, no tetanus shot. But hey, I'm not bitter. Sure, with a fully functioning thumb, I could have been a concert violinist. Yeah, I could have played shortstop for the Yankees. But I had other things on my mind. Like not being a wimp.

Pantywaist kids today are afraid of anything sharp for fear they might "poke their eyes out." Really? Sharp objects were the only toys I played with. For that, I have to give my mom credit. She recognized that I had an uncanny aptitude for excessive bleeding. So she bought me all kinds of sharp objects and gave me loads of unsupervised time to experiment with them. Like the time I was using a claw hammer to pound a nail into an exceedingly hard piece of lumber. Lightweight twerps today would have gotten discouraged and started playing video games. Not me. No stinking piece of wood was going to kick my butt. So I grabbed the hammer with both hands and reared back. I whipped that hammer over my head with such force that the claw end banged smack into the top of my skull, leaving a red crater where my cowlick used to be.

I dabbed at the crown of my head, felt a huge divot, and saw blood on my hand. By now I knew better than to run crying like a mama's boy to you know who. And I needed iodine like I needed a hole in the head. So I gutted it out. You know why? Cause, unlike these yellow-bellied cream puffs today, I'm not a weakling. I'm not afraid of a whack in the cranium with a claw hammer. Besides, I looked on the bright side. Thereafter, I was able to store loose change and Corn Nuts in the indentation on my head.

Back when, I didn't have time to waste thinking about trivial matters like injuries. I was too busy getting hurt to worry about not getting hurt. If I wasn't dead, I'd slap on a Band-Aid, and get over it. And you don't hear me complaining, do you?

WHAT'S IN A NAME?

I WAS AT THE SAN JOSE Jazz Festival with my friend,
Wilner. We waited near the main outdoor stage, where
we were supposed to meet Louis. But Louis hadn't
shown up yet. Annoyed, Wilner whipped out his cell.

"Louis, where you at?"

"I haven't left yet."

"Haven't left yet!? Man, you better get your butt down
here! I'm here with my boy; he gonna kick your ass!"

"Who's gonna kick my ass? What's his name?"

"Brian."

"Brian!? That ain't even a bad man's name. Brian's not
the name of someone who kicks your ass. It's the name of
the guy who greets you at Costco."

Okay, I admit it. When it comes to intimidating names,
Brian is on the wimpy end of the spectrum. It might have
something to do with the *Br–* consonant cluster at the
beginning. There must be a psychological effect when it
comes to certain sounds. That's why guys in the Mafia
aren't named Bradley or Bruce. They're named Nick and
Tony. You never see mob films where a couple of saps
hiding out in an abandoned warehouse are struck with
fear after receiving a phone call from a hitman whose name
starts with *Br–*.

"Stash the loot! Bradley's on his way!"

"You mean Brandon's little brother!?"

If my Sicilian mother had her way, my name would have been Vinnie or Carmine. But my Irish dad overruled her and gave me an Irish name. I guess I should be grateful I wasn't named Seamus or Declan or Fergus. I almost was.

In those days before ultrasound tests, parents never knew the gender of a child until the kid was born. So most parents-to-be picked out a girl and a boy name. If I was a girl, my name was supposed to be Kelly, an Irish name that can be used for both genders. Thankfully, when I came out of the womb, I looked more like a Brian than a Kelly. Had I been named Kelly, the Tonys and Nicks of the world would have been issued a lifetime license to bully me. To harass a guy named Brian you only have to renew your license every four years.

My Sicilian uncle and godfather, John La Duca, recognized that my name lacked panache. He decided the best way to address the problem was to give me a nickname. Uncle Johnny—or The Duke, as he was known in The City—owned Duke's Barber Shop in San Francisco. The Duke took me with him to his barber shop every chance he got, to toughen me up, and allow me to make a few bucks shining shoes. So that I could feel like I had some spunk, he took to calling me Little Duke.

Who would mess with a kid nicknamed Little Duke? Answer: Two kids from the Excelsior neighborhood who shined shoes regularly at Duke's.

The first time they saw me working the barber shop, I was eight years old and completely lacking in street smarts. They caught me in the act of polishing a wingtip and muscled in on either side of me, scrutinizing my technique. They communicated with each other in telepathic code, tacitly detailing the methods they would use to dismember me.

The oldest of the two spoke. "Man, what's your name?"

"Little Duke," I said, buffing a toe cap to a fine sheen.

"**Little** Duke?"

"I'm the Duke's nephew."

Both of them glanced at The Duke to confirm whether this white boy was messing with them or telling the truth. My uncle just nodded and continued trimming a sideburn.

Once they discovered that I was family, these inner city kids let their guards down and gave me a pass. For the rest of the morning, while we hung out, talking baseball and sharing shoe shining secrets, I was Little Duke. Had I told them my real name was Brian, I would have been dead by noon.

Back home in San Jose, I assumed my true identity as Brian, a Catholic kid with good manners and a cowlick. Sure, every couple of months, in the presence of my godfather, I could pose as Little Duke, a city kid with moxie. But who was I kidding? I was never gonna be a Nick or a Tony, or kick anybody's ass at a jazz festival. It just wasn't in my nature. But with a name like Brian, I knew that with a little luck, one day I might be able to get a job at Costco.

I DUPED THE DMV

WE WERE DRIVING SOUTH OUT of the Tulsa airport in a rented car driven by sixty-year driving veteran, Bill Cleveland. Abruptly, Bill slammed on the brakes and laid on the horn, gesturing wildly at the confused driver in front of us who had come to a dead stop to read a series of signs directing drivers out of the airport parking lot.

"Now, Bill," reasoned Barbara, Bill's wife, "she's just an old lady."

"Little old ladies shouldn't be driving!" Bill snapped back.

I tell this story as a cautionary tale for those of you who believe you will never be involved in such a scenario. I stand before you as living proof. A mere twenty years have passed since that afternoon in Oklahoma. I have become that little old lady.

When I drive, I make it a point to maintain the speed limit. This causes traffic jams wherever I go. Out of courtesy, I stick to the slow lane. But cars zoom past me at speeds in excess of 90 miles an hour, so that I feel like I'm sitting in a parked car. I cling tenaciously to my outmoded driving values, like the last of a dying breed. What can I say? I'm a throwback. I insist on signaling before turning or changing lanes. Last December I signaled and a guy rolled down his

71

window to compliment me. He thought my blinker was a Christmas display.

I became acutely aware of my transformation from virile young man to decrepit old bag this past September, a month before my birthday. I received an official notice requiring me to appear in person at the DMV to renew my driver's license. Cool, I thought, here's an opportunity to get an updated photo on my license that reflects my accurate age and maturity. I've had so many consecutive renewals by mail that my current photo is from when I was eight.

So I went online, and, using my advanced technological skills, navigated the website of the DMV, which is maintained by a Siberian agency that employs indentured servants in Bangalore, India. By some stroke of luck, I was able to successfully schedule an appointment after a mere sixteen hours online, at a convenient time that would give me twelve minutes from the time my school was dismissed until I was due at the DMV. Fortunately for me, Wren, who is capable of driving at speeds over the posted speed limit, drove, and got me to the DMV with thirty seconds to spare.

I arrived with the smug cockiness of a Hollywood celebrity who enters a top shelf restaurant without a reservation. I knew all I had to do was breeze into the joint, inform a helpful paper shuffler that I had an appointment, and I would be waited on by an army of civil servants, whose only desire was to make my DMV experience a pleasant one.

Welcome to a government-run agency in the new millennium. Instead of encountering a friendly Walmart style greeter at the door, I logjammed into a double line of stressed out neurotics who resembled rejects from the casting call of *One Flew Over the Cuckoo's Nest*. The lines extended all the way out the door. After a twenty minute wait, the two lines merged into a single counter where a bureaucracy-scarred veteran confirmed appointments, answered queries and defused volatile confrontations.

While waiting in line, I finally understood why the roads are such a frenetic mess. Just look around. They let anybody drive. All you gotta do is pass a test and they set you loose on the roads. There oughta be a law.

When I finally advanced to the front of the line, I was given a ticket, like the kind you get in a bakery. Only, I was pretty sure I wouldn't be leaving with a German chocolate cake. To my pleasant surprise, within a minute, my number flashed on an electronic screen that instructed me to proceed to Window 11.

I smiled at my good fortune and strode straight up to the window where a smiling, friendly DMV employee assisted me cheerfully. Except that he wasn't smiling. And he wasn't cheerful. And he wasn't very friendly. But he was a DMV employee—I think. And he did assist me. He barked out a request for my license and paperwork, and in a semi-audible voice asked me for thirty-five dollars, which I paid gladly as the privilege for driving on gridlocked streets and contributing to the demise of the planet.

After I handed over a check, he gestured halfheartedly to an eye chart over his left shoulder and told me to cover my right eye and read the chart aloud. No sweat. I covered my right eye and rattled off the letters perfectly. A rush of pride washed over me as I realized I was acing this test. Things cannot get much better than this, I thought.

And boy was I right. Cause the next thing I knew Mr. Civil Servant pointed to a different eye chart a few feet away and asked me to read from it with my other eye. Piece of cake. I covered my left eye and focused on the chart. But all the letters blurred together. Were those even letters?

Hieroglyphics? Emojis? What was this, some kind of Jedi mind trick? With my right eye, I couldn't tell an E from a B, an R from a P, an O from a Q, an S from a Z. Fortunately, my buddy behind the counter was preoccupied with a word search or something equally as fascinating, and hadn't made eye contact with me once since the test began. So I did what I had to do. I cheated.

Like a skilled prestidigitator, I lifted the hand covering my eye slightly to the left, just enough so that I could see with my good eye. I started to recite the letters and I was on a roll. But right in the middle of my well-orchestrated ruse, Deputy DMV snapped his head in my direction and studied me with hawklike attention. As soon as he did, I slapped my hand back over my eye so hard it left a bruise. Again, the letters blurred, as the civil servant scrutinized me. I cleared my throat to stall for time. He eventually got bored and returned to his word search. As soon as he looked down, I lifted my left hand again, let my good eye do its stuff, and passed the exam with flying colors.

A month later, my new license arrived in the mail. The photograph shows the winning smile of a distinguished elderly gentleman with a touch of gray and two eyes that appear deceptively younger than the birthdate listed. My new license doesn't expire for another four years. By that time, I'm hoping they'll grant me an extension by mail. Barring an investigation into an eye chart cheating scandal, I may have made my final visit to the DMV.

I'll be honest, I'm not proud of what I did. But what's the big deal? All right, so I don't see well at night, my distance vision is shot, my depth perception is iffy. My wife swears I'm color blind and can't tell the difference between red and green. And I'm basically blind in one eye. But at least I have a valid driver's license.

READING, WRITING, AND REVOLVERS

A S OF YESTERDAY, I'M FINALLY convinced that I retired from teaching at the right time. After yet another school shooting, gun rights advocates have proposed the insane idea that the most effective way to deal with these increasingly commonplace incidents is to put guns in the hands of teachers.

I can see it now: It's the first day of a new school year. Bright-eyed, open-minded students with butterflies in their stomachs file into the classroom, anxious to meet their new teacher.

"Good morning, class! My name is Mr. Conroy. I'm looking forward to an exciting year of academic achievement and personal growth. But before we get into all that Kumbaya crap, Say hello to my little friend!"

Teachers with guns. Why didn't we think of this before? This could solve so many of our problems. Discipline issues would become non-existent. Instead of after-school detention, we can simply line kids up before a firing squad and shoot the trouble makers. Question authority—yo, question this! Wear a hoodie—oops! I didn't know you were just raising your hand. Move over, Finland. American test scores are about to skyrocket.

Forget about novels and notebooks, math manipulatives,

and lab equipment. Curricular materials like that are a thing of the past. Thanks to the technology of military-grade weapons, students can now learn by staring down the barrel of a gun. Never mind that the typical teacher lacks the temperament to handle a gun, much less the ability to kill an intruder. While I don't have the evidence to prove it, I'm thinking more teachers would be willing to take a bullet for their students, than would be willing to fire a bullet.

If we require teachers to carry guns, within a year or two, the profession would lose thousands of empathetic individuals, gifted at organizing learning environments. I can say unequivocally, that if I were forced to carry a gun in my classroom, I would be forced to resign. For thirty-five years my goal was to keep my students safe. Something I was able to accomplish every year — without a gun. The very act of carrying a gun in the classroom would compromise my values to the extent that I would no longer be the same teacher.

"Mr. Conroy, are you going to wear that gun on your hip all year long?"

"Sure as shootin'! My job is to keep you young'uns safe."

"But...wouldn't having a gun in the classroom make us less safe? I mean, what about the potential for your firearm to discharge accidentally, or the possibility that one of us might get ahold of your gun, or even that you might shoot one of us in a fit of rage?"

"Hey, let's not go off half-cocked. I'm a trained teacher. I may have a lapsed credential, but I went through a six-hour training to obtain my gun permit. Last weekend I even practiced at the shooting range, where I shot at a paper diagram of the human anatomy and hit the target almost half the time. And if you're insinuating trying to steal my gun and use my weapon against me, all I can say is, Go ahead, make my day!"

"Mr. Conroy, will any of this be on the test?"

"You must be gunnin' for an A! Yes, it will be on the test. The test of life. The sooner you snowflakes learn that the world isn't some amusement park full of Good Samaritans looking out for your best interests, the better off you'll be. It's a cold, cruel world out there and you need to arm yourselves against the dark forces of evil. The only thing protecting you from these dark forces is a good guy with a gun. Now get to work before this good guy has to teach you a lesson!"

Yes, the good old days of education may be coming to an end. As the old cliché reminds us, teachers don't kill learning, people kill learning. People who think guns don't kill people. People who are currently trying to kill our education system by deluding themselves into believing that more guns will make us safer, that we can never prevent school shootings, that a firearm is an educational tool.

I'm sure that, deep down in their holsters, gun owners have good hearts. And, I know they care about their children. But on this issue, they're out of their depth. They're too quick on the trigger. They need to let teachers do what we do. Let us do our jobs, and we'll let you folks keep your guns. Even though we know the world would be a safer place without them.

RUNS IN THE FAMILY

EVERY SUNDAY MORNING, I USED to take a long, leisurely run with my brother Rob. We'd venture out to a rugged trail in the mountains, or a shaded path in the foothills. Or we'd set out to conquer some killer hill that would have destroyed lesser mortals. Sometimes we'd just stick to the familiarity of the paved creek trail, halfway between our houses. I could make it through rough weeks, knowing that on Sunday, my brother and I would lace up our shoes and run our hearts out, rain or shine.

We were like the US Postal Service. Neither snow nor rain nor heat nor gloom of night stopped us from our Sunday morning run. Thick fog, pounding rain, hundred-degree heat—nothing fazed us. If it was freezing cold, we just toughed it out.

Once, we ran from Los Gatos to Saratoga in weather so bone-chillingly cold, every moving body part was numb or arthritic and tiny icicles hung from our chins. By the time we reached Saratoga, our jaws were frozen solid. Our articulation was so unintelligible, neither of us knew what the hell the other was saying. We kept blabbing on, though, convinced that if we kept yakking nonstop, we could save our lips from frostbite. We sounded like two drunks after an all-night bender. Since I couldn't understand a word my brother said, after a while, instead of continually asking him to repeat himself, I just agreed with anything he said.

The next morning I discovered I had agreed to give him the pink slip to my Honda.

When Rob and I first began our Sunday runs, I was in my late thirties. I took it for granted that we'd be doing this well into our advanced years. Now that those advanced years have officially arrived, I have to take responsibility for the fact that, were it not for some unbelievably bad judgment on my part, we would still be running together.

Let me give you a little context on my oldest brother. First, he's the nicest guy in the world. He's not someone who holds a grudge, but the guy's got a memory like an elephant. As a result, he holds me personally responsible for triggering his incurable case of PTRD—Post Traumatic Running Disorder. It's not something he obsesses over. It's just that he refuses to run with me on Sundays—or any other day of the week.

I think it all began on the day we ran the San Francisco Half Marathon in Golden Gate Park. As we drove up to the race, I told him I knew the perfect place to park, a couple blocks from the start line. And sure enough, we found an ideal parking space on Irving at 18th Street, a couple minute's walk from the start.

After the race, we found that the course doesn't loop back and return to where it began. The finish line is way out to hell and gone on the Great Highway, near 48th Street. So now that we're beyond the point of exhaustion, dehydrated, hungry, oxygen and electrolyte deprived, I force my brother to walk thirty city blocks back to our perfect parking space. While we walked back to the car in silence, he plotted my murder in meticulous detail, all the while searching for a convenient dumpster where he could stash my body. The following Sunday he informed me he couldn't make it to our weekly run. He said he had to attend an anger management class to suppress some violent impulses he'd been experiencing for the past week.

Fortunately, we were able to patch things up without any bloodshed, and we got back to our Sunday runs. A couple years later, I had learned my lesson about races that begin and end in different places. So one day when we ran the local Great Race, we drove two cars. I parked my car near the finish line. Then Rob drove us in his car to the start line, where I took off my warmup sweats with my car keys in the pockets, and locked them in his car. After the race, we jogged a couple of blocks to my car, only to find that my keys were in another zip code. Luckily, the keys weren't thirty blocks away this time. They were only four miles away. Down a dangerously narrow highway. With cars zooming by at sixty miles an hour. I told my brother to look on the bright side. At least he had his little brother with him to shoot the breeze. But I don't think the breeze was the only thing he wanted to shoot.

And then there was that beautiful morning at Lake Merced in San Francisco. Against his better judgment, he agreed to run the Christmas Relays. It'll be fun, I promised. You'll be part of a team of four runners. Each person runs a single loop around the lake. What could go wrong?

Rob's first two teammates made it around the lake in decent time. But halfway through the third leg, the sky darkened, and angry clouds gathered. The third runner crossed the finish line and handed off to Rob, who lit out like a man half his age. About ten minutes later, the sky opened up, and dumped a monsoon on him.

Most runners couldn't care less about a little rain. But this stuff pounded down in biblical proportion. We expected Noah to appear, hurrying pairs of runners from different age divisions onboard his ark. Even the most fearless runners ran for cover. In minutes, the race course cleared and there were few signs of life. Runners who had already finished, hopped in their cars and sped off, without waiting for their teammates. They figured, screw this. I signed up for a run, not a swim.

But not me. I waited patiently for my brother. In the warmth and safety of a heated car. With windshield wipers. I'm nothing, if not loyal. Especially when it comes to family. I know that blood is thicker than water. But with this water slamming down so hard, I couldn't be absolutely certain.

By the time my brother waded through the finish line, he was unrecognizable. He looked like a muskrat who'd swum in from Alaska. I tried to keep a straight face, but I couldn't help laughing. Apparently Rob failed to see the humor. We were supposed to be enjoying the spirit of the Christmas Relays, but he was shivering like the Grinch and couldn't wait to get the hell out of there.

That year Rob got a cold for Christmas,…and an ugly sweater. He blamed me for both. Things went sour from then on. For his New Year's resolution, he vowed never to run with me again.

I miss those Sunday morning runs. These days the only time I run with my brother is when he's chasing me. That's why I've got to stay in shape. It could be a matter of life and death. Still, I envision a day when Rob will put the past behind him, and together we'll drive out to a race on a beautiful Sunday morning, with not even a cloud in the sky. I know the perfect place to park.

LILY COPS A BUZZ

T HE OTHER DAY, AFTER WREN and I returned from walking our dog, Lily, we noticed she was acting hella strange. As soon as we opened the door, Lily staggered to her doggie bed, flopped on its foam cushion, and remained there in a comatose state. That alone wouldn't have sounded any alarms, but for the next half hour, the poor pup began to moan in a manner that could only suggest she was having great sex or was in great distress. Surmising it was the latter, we rushed her to an emergency vet.

After a battery of tests, the bespectacled vet explained that, based on the dog's lethargy, her dilated pupils, her slowed reactions, and the skunky smell emanating from every pore, Lily had ingested marijuana. And, in his expert opinion, it was some killer shit.

Where Lily scored the weed is anyone's guess. Likely some careless high school stoner dropped a bud while retrieving his cell phone from his stash pocket. As the space cadet continues down the street, texting obliviously, we happen to pass by on our afternoon walk. Lily catches a whiff of the overpowering scent of sensimilla on the sidewalk, sniffs it, and, while we're checking out the blossoms of a plum tree, she inhales the entire bud. (Though she later swears that she never inhaled.) Next thing we know, Lily's baked like a cake on the Fourth of July.

The doctor assures us there's nothing to get uptight about. He recommends we take Lily home, have her kick back on the waterbed, and watch Cheech and Chong movies until the effects wear off. On the way back from the vet, we stop and score three bags of Mr. Barky's Vegetarian Dog Biscuits, a frisbee, and a tie-dyed neck scarf. So that Lily feels mellow, we play Grateful Dead jams all the way back to the pad, which works like a charm, because she promptly crashes out. Or maybe that was just her way of telling us she thought the music sucked.

Once we get home, Lily fetches our Bob Marley's Greatest Hits CD, holds it in her mouth, and starts jabbing it against our legs. She keeps bugging us until we put the CD on and crank it up to eleven. For the next couple of hours, her bark is slurred. Worst of all, she smiles inappropriately at things we don't find funny at all. She must have had a wicked case of the munchies because she polished off a whole bag of Mr. Barky's Biscuits before zonking out with her mouth wide open.

Now that recreational marijuana has been legalized in California, incidents involving stoned pets are bound to increase exponentially. As a responsible pet owner, you can ensure your dog's health and safety by keeping an eye out for low lying ganja. And making sure to change your dog's bong water every day.

PAMELA ANDERSON DIGS SKINNY VEGETARIAN GUYS

I WOKE UP IN A SWEAT, thinking of Pamela Anderson. She stood before me, intimidatingly large, wearing a skimpy bikini, like the woman in the poster for *Attack of the 50 Foot Woman*. Only Pamela's glistening green bikini was made entirely out of lettuce. What's gotten into you, Pamela?

A vegetarian lifestyle — that's what's gotten into her. Our girl Pamela has converted to vegetarianism and become an animal activist. Ever since, PETA, People for the Ethical Treatment of Animals, recruited her as their poster child. To capitalize on her ample charms as a sex symbol, they fitted her in a bikini, made out of three lettuce leaves, that conformed perfectly to the contours of her curvaceous anatomy. Some lucky camera nerd got to photograph extreme close-ups of Pamela. The photos were then enlarged, and subsequently projected onto massive electronic billboards in Times Square with the caption: *Turn Over a New Leaf: Try Vegetarian*. Then, for the benefit of we mere mortals who didn't happen to be in Manhattan for the original screening, the photos were published in PETA's monthly publications.

I don't know if you've seen the literature PETA sends out to its members, but they are as close as you can get to vegetarian porn. Seriously, in what other magazine can you find vegan recipes, pictures of animals being abused in laboratories, and glossy photographs of sex goddesses like Pamela Anderson, all on the same page?

Apparently there are a ton of hot Hollywood babes these days who are animal activists and vegetarians. Because they're on every page of the PETA periodicals. And evidently they swear by lifestyles that are completely natural. That's why most of them have had boob jobs and plastic surgery.

But hey, if it takes hot Hollywood babes to convert the macho meat-eating men of America to vegetarianism, then I'm all for it. I mean, you have to hit people where they live. No straight, working class guy is gonna even look twice at some longhaired New Agey dude holding a sign urging him to refuse to buy his wife that fur coat he's saved for years to buy. But put a sign in Pamela Anderson's hands that says, *Nothing Comes Between Me and My Faux Fur*, and suddenly you got the guy thinking. See, PETA figured out that no man wants to be told he's a bad boy if he's not a vegetarian. Unless he's told he's a bad boy by that naughty vegetarian, Elvira, Mistress of the Dark. In which case the conversion can occur far more rapidly.

The possibilities for the mass conversion of society to a meatless diet are infinite now, thanks to the visionary work of PETA. I foresee a time in the future when there will be a Baywatch spinoff, in which well-endowed meat-free women and buff plant-based men rescue unhealthy people, just as they're about to drown in oceans of junk food.

I can see it now: The title sequence flashes across the screen, underscored by the theme music to another episode of *Pamela Anderson, Vegetarian Lifeguard*. The opening shot is of a sparkling, white sand beach in Southern California. Close up of a rugged looking muscle man who has just devoured his third Big Mac in a row. As he chews the last bite, suddenly his arteries constrict. A pain shoots up the left side of his body. He clutches at his heart, but it's too late. He crumples in a heap on the hot sand, the victim of a massive stroke.

The camera pans to a nearby sweep of beach where Pamela Anderson, Vegetarian Lifeguard, sits atop her lifeguard tower like a queen. She senses distress, turns in the direction of the fallen macho man, and swings into action. She sprints straight into the path of the camera in what appears to be a suspended motion that accentuates her sculpted muscles. As the camera tracks her movements, her bulging bazongoes bounce sensually, struggling to stay within the confines of the silky fabric of her red thong one-piece. But incredibly, her uniform remains intact, as she reaches the muscle-bound stroke victim in record time.

With erotic dexterity, she lays his body flat on the shimmering sand, elevates his head voluptuously, clears a chunk of Big Mac from his mouth, and administers CPR. A split second later, the Assistant Vegetarian Lifeguard arrives, bearing a striking resemblance to David Hasselhoff. He kneels on the sand and counts out loud, matching the rhythm of Pamela's heaving breasts, while her steamy lips breathe life into the dying meat eater.

Miraculously, after only a few moments, the macho man regains consciousness and begins to breathe of his own accord. His eyes open slowly, and to his pleasant surprise, he finds himself gazing into the breathtakingly beautiful eyes of Pamela Anderson, Vegetarian Lifeguard, the same woman he's been trying to impress for years by pumping iron on this beach. Overcome with gratitude for saving his life, he stammers the only meaningful words he can utter at a time like this, "Are you...free tonight?"

Pamela Anderson parts her full collagen-enhanced lips seductively and replies in a breathy whisper, "Sorry. I have plans."

In a jump cut, the camera frames a medium close-up of Pamela's boyfriend. Not a tattooed, mohawked member of an eighties hair band, but a 98-pound vegetarian. He extends a holistic hand to Pamela. She stands, joins hands with her soulmate, and they stroll along the beach, fingers interlaced, disappearing beneath the setting sun.

The final shot is of the muscle man, sitting on the beach, all by himself. He shakes his head in regret at what could have been, making a mental note to give up junk food and go meatless. Before the credits roll, we hear him say, "Damn! Those vegetarian guys always get the chicks."

It could happen.

GLOSSARY FOR AGING BABY BOOMERS

Whats happening, Baby Boomers? If you, like me, have recently joined the geriatric generation, you should know that several words and phrases that were part of the lexicon of the 60s have taken on a new connotation now that you're in your 60s. To save you the embarrassment of sounding like an idiot at your local senior center, I share with you this brief glossary.

Age of Aquarius:
The minimum age to qualify for AARP membership.

Be-in:
The time you should be off the streets and home in bed, preferably by 7:30 pm each evening.

Catch some rays:
Get a CT scan.

Free love:
When you look so pathetic that strangers say, "Looks like someone needs a hug."

Get it on:
Ability to put on underwear without pulling a muscle.

Give peace a chance:
Eat more roughage.

Grass:
That crap in the front yard you need to mow.

Hash:
Comes with eggs any style on the senior menu at Denny's.

Heavy, man!:
You need to lose twenty pounds.

I hear you:
I just turned on my hearing aid.

I'm hip:
Now that I've had my hip replaced, I can walk again.

Letting it all hang out:
Sitting on the recliner in boxer shorts.

Longhairs:
Untrimmed nose hair.

LSD:
Low sodium diet.

Making the scene:
Getting to the movie theater for the senior discount matinee.

Mellow out:
Take two Ambien.

My old lady:
The senior citizen I married.

Outtasight:
Too far to see without progressive lenses.

Rock out:
Got my kidney stone removed.

Roll a joint:
Messed up my knee again.

Score:
Get meds at the pharmacy.

Turn on, tune in, drop out:
Grab the remote, switch to ESPN, and fall asleep.

Twister:
A chiropractor.

What a trip!:
The wife and I took a cruise to the Bahamas.

What's your bag?:
Is that your catheter?

NOT A HAPPY CAMPER

T HERE'S NOTHING QUITE LIKE THE joy of camping. Kicking back in the great outdoors, the way it was meant to be. Fresh air, sunshine, cool running streams. Immersed in nature with nothing to disturb the serenity, except a fellow camper's radio blasting heavy metal, or the buzz of ten thousand mosquitoes. Where your only regret is that you didn't purchase more Doritos and Budweiser back at the convenience store thirty miles down the road. Ah, it doesn't get much better than that.

Whenever I think about camping, my thoughts hearken back to those halcyon days of my youth. Back to those days when the environment was pristine. When the air was unpolluted, when a man was free to dump toxic sludge into a river, and when pesticides sweetened our fruits and vegetables.

As a youngster, raised in suburbia, I grew up wanting nothing more than to commune with nature. Fortunately, there was a campground not far from my home in the nearby foothills, called Saratoga Springs. One day, when I was 12 or 13, I discovered that I could camp there all by myself if I had parental permission. As an example of how much our world has changed, I asked my mom if I could camp over night with a friend at the campground. You'd think she might be concerned that I would be kidnapped by the Charles Manson cult, but no, she agreed without argument.

(After each camping trip over the next few years, I would return safe and sound, much to her disappointment.)

A couple days later, my buddy and I rode our stingray bikes, with those long, narrow banana seats, about seven miles to the campground. Our sleeping bags were jammed in between the handlebars; our backpacks, stuffed with junk food, were slung across our backs. We looked like bikers from *Easy Rider* (the version where the bikers don't get shot by rednecks). In our pockets we carried the tickets to our emancipation: folded up, handwritten notes from our parents:

> *To Whom It May Concern,*
>
> *My son Brian has permission to camp overnight at Saratoga Springs Campground on June 23rd, 1968.*
>
> *Signed,*
>
> *His Mother,*
> *Sally Conroy*

Once we arrived at the campground, we presented our notes to the owner, and we were free. Free to do whatever we wanted with no parental supervision. We played out our Davy Crocket and Daniel Boone fantasies, roughing it in the great outdoors, where the buffalo roam, or at least squirrels roam. We submerged our cans of root beer in the stream beside our campsite to keep them cool. And just like early pioneers did, we ate cans of Hormel Chili con Carne for dinner, cooked over an open fire. Then we roasted marshmallows and played cards late into the night. When it was pitch dark we fell asleep beneath the redwoods, with the earth for a pillow and the stars for a blanket. For a thirteen-year-old, this was living large.

* * *

By the time I married Wren, I hadn't camped for several years. One day we were reminiscing about the good old days when we used to hike and camp and have sex under the stars on full moon nights. (I may have invented that last part, but don't tell Wren.) In a moment of inspired lunacy, we hatched a plan to go camping. We would take to the open road and find a rustic campground, far from the electronic hum of Silicon Valley, out in nature where we belong.

This took place during a time when I was well-established in my teaching career, and had a little disposable income to invest on camping equipment. Hey, we figured, if we're going to do this thing, let's do it right. So we made the rounds to rugged sounding outlets for rugged individuals: REI, Any Mountain, The North Face, Mel Cotton's. We spent hundreds of dollars on state-of-the-art camping gear. Sleeping bags made from top-of-the-line microfibers. Inflatable air mattresses. A lightweight dome tent. A Coleman stove with pots, pans, and utensils. A compact cooler complete with ice packs. With all of this equipment we were guaranteed to have the optimum camping experience.

Then we set about scheduling our trip. Gone were the days when you could simply pull in to a campground on a moment's notice. Now you had to call a 1-800 number and make reservations months in advance. No problemo. The folks who took our reservations were friendly and helpful and played us lovely muzak while they put us on hold for forty-two minutes.

After extensive research, we settled on Julia Pfeiffer State Park in Big Sur. We consulted the Farmer's Almanac to select the ideal three days in June when the weather would be warm, yet still mild; and when the stars would be cosmically aligned and most visible in the sky. The reservations were made, our equipment was brand new, and our hearts were in the highlands.

When June rolled around, we drove the Coast Highway from Santa Cruz to Big Sur, taking the scenic route so we could enjoy the journey, rather than merely the destination. As we drove, we saw the waves breaking onto the shore. There was excitement in the air, and excrement on the windshield, thanks to the seagulls.

We arrived at the state park, checked in, and were directed to our campsite. We got to work like pros, setting up camp as if we knew what we were doing: Erecting our tent, unrolling our sleeping bags, inflating the air mattresses, priming our stove, positioning our cooler, pig proofing our food, unfolding our lawn chairs. And then we sat down and took a well-deserved rest. And listened to the crickets.

By the next afternoon we were bored stiff. We'd taken three hikes, and played every card game ever invented. We were going to play strip poker, but we were afraid the mosquitoes would eat us alive. Even dinner, fresh from a can of Amy's Kitchen Vegetarian Organic Refried Beans cooked over an open fire, failed to excite us. Everything seemed so loud. Radios, siblings quarreling, frat boys on summer break. The crickets were driving me crazy; I wanted to tell them to shut the hell up. The incessant yap of the bluejays was getting on my nerves big time. Even trees were starting to piss me off.

Wren and I began to reminisce about the good old days

when we vacationed in the tranquility of a hotel room, with cable television and room service, where we could gaze out the window at trees. Disillusioned, we scanned our shabby campsite with disdain, wondering what we'd gotten ourselves into. Right about the time I was ready to chuck our new Coleman lantern at the next friggin' bluejay who squawked, Wren and I arrived at a tacit agreement: Let's get the hell outta Dodge!

The next morning we broke camp at the crack of dawn, before the blue jays had a chance to jeer at our predawn getaway. We tossed our gear into the car haphazardly and floored it back to the asphalt forests of San Jose.

Twenty years later the camping equipment is collecting dust in a dark corner of an overhead cabinet in our garage, where, unless there's an apocalypse, it will never see the light of day.

Don't get me wrong. I love nature, I just don't want to sleep with it. I like to admire it from the fifth story window of a hotel room, where the only thing to disturb the serenity is the rattle of an air conditioner and the hum of a television, the way nature intended it.

IN MY HUMBLE OPINION

A S I SIT DOWN TO write this, I have to LOL. Oh, sorry. Where are my manners? Just in case you've been living in a Third World cave since the advent of email and texting, let me explain. LOL is an abbreviation used by tech-savvy geeks who never laugh out loud. Techies utilize LOL as a time saving method of calling attention to something that's not funny to begin with, and becomes even less funny when they tell you how funny it is.

Before you make the assumption that I'm a bitter old fossil who believes that the English language has suffered immeasurably as a result of reducing communication to a series of abbreviations and acronyms, let me be perfectly honest: You are absolutely correct. I hate texting acronyms! They drive me up the wall. Now, I can feel your thumbs starting to twitch: Dude, OMG! IMHO UR my BFF, but WTF? RU a technophobe? JK. CU L8R, bruh. ROTFL.

If you are the author of the above message, never do that again. It's true, I don't look very smart, but I can read actual spelled-out words fluently. Furthermore, as a person who prefers the English language in its unabridged version, let me do you the favor of dissecting your message.

First things first. Dude, I just met you three weeks ago. It's kind of a stretch to say that we're **Best Friends Forever.** Certainly it's possible we'll be friends until the end of time. But if you don't stop with the acronyms ASAP, our friendship will be severely abbreviated.

OMG: Since when is God yours exclusively, and when did you suddenly become so religious that you have to invoke God in every email or text? For God's sake, give it a rest.

IMHO? No. You've lost the right to consider yourself and your opinion humble once you've stated that you're humble. That's no longer humility; it's imbecility. Not to mention: pretentious. If you want to be humble, be humble. But don't tell anyone about it.

RU: Seriously? Does omitting four measly letters really save that much time? You must be very busy. So much for technology saving everyone huge amounts of time. But I could never convince you of this irony. Know Y? B/C UR an idiot.

What the F is **WTF** about? If you want to use the F-word, just use the friggin' F-word. There's nothing quite as satisfying as the percussive – *ck* sound at the end of the F-word. Merely saying F doesn't cut it. But, hey, what the F do I know?

CU sounds like the University I was never smart enough to get into. Good thing, because all of the graduates from CU are computer nerds who end their texts and emails with TTYL. If you are a CU graduate, I have no desire to CU, so FU.

JK...Oh, you're kidding? Now I get it. I'm so glad you told me. It's almost like having a digital laugh track. If you hadn't clued me in to the fact that you were kidding, I wouldn't be laughing out loud right now.

Rolling On The Floor Laughing? Come on! When was the last time, outside of a looney bin, that you actually saw someone rolling on the floor laughing? Unless you're

Richard Pryor, you probably don't have the ability to make an audience roll on the floor laughing. And even with Pryor, one of the great comedians of our time, it wasn't only the jokes that made his cocaine-addled audiences roll on the floor.

L8R? There's nothing I H8 more than abbreviations that combine letters and numbers: W8, B4, 2moro. There should be a special place for people who believe it's acceptable to mangle the English language like this: the penitentiary. A place where these miscreants can text to their heart's content, far removed from literate society. Which is likely where I'll end up. In the penitentiary, not literate society. Because I'm gonna strangle the next slacker who sends me a message in texting code!

PLZ, NXT time U want 2 TXT me, spell UR words out. Is that 2 much 2 ask? GR8! LOL. (Not!)

HOT AND SPICY

S EVERAL YEARS AGO, I DECIDED to switch to a new doctor at a smaller facility about a mile from home. An unsightly rash had developed on my stomach. But I didn't panic. As a rational human being, not wanting to jump to conclusions, I merely assumed I had contracted a flesh-eating disease and that my death was imminent.

So I took potluck and scheduled an appointment with a doctor who was available the following day. The next morning, I fidgeted anxiously as I waited for the doctor in the examination room. When she arrived, I found her pleasant enough. She introduced herself and performed routine medical examinations. She looked in my ears, ostensibly to ensure there were no potatoes growing there; she listened to my heart—always a catchy beat; and she examined the scum on my tongue. Then she enquired as to the purpose of my visit. I explained in a calm, detached manner that a rash was ravaging my flesh. She scrutinized the rash, and poked my abdomen to ensure that all my internal organs were in the proper place. Then she removed her glasses, and sighed with clinical certainty.

"What's your diagnosis, doctor?"

"You need to stop eating spicy foods." With that, she forced a smile, took a couple steps toward the door and asked, "Did you have any other questions?"

"Uh,…Yes," I said. "Just one small question: Where did

you study medicine? At the Culinary Institute? How could you have possibly arrived at this diagnosis when you never asked me a single question about my diet? Spicy foods? I never even eat spicy foods, you quack!"

Actually, I think my exact words were, "No,...no questions."

Needless to say, that was my one and only appointment with that doctor, whose name I have long forgotten. See, my problem with doctors is that they lump everyone together into the same category. They've learned through years of experience that the average person overindulges in spicy foods, causing them to break out in mysterious rashes. But not this average person. For forty-five years I've been a vegetarian. My diet is unbelievably bland. As the chef in our home, rainbow quinoa, lentils and kale is about as spicy as I get. I don't even salt my foods, for crying out loud. Which might explain why our closest friends always have pressing emergencies to attend to whenever we invite them for dinner.

It wasn't always this way. Having been raised by a Sicilian mother, garlic found its way into every dish we ate growing up. I'm not just talking about spaghetti and eggplant parmesan, either. Mom put garlic in tapioca pudding and lime jello. I was twelve years old before I discovered that other moms didn't add crushed garlic to hot chocolate.

Years later, when I encountered Buddhism, I learned that strict Mahayana Buddhists avoid eating onions and garlic, because they stir up the blood and increase sexual desire. All those years I thought my hot blood and incomparable sex drive was just a Sicilian thing. Who knew?

Our family used to eat antipasto with our meals on a regular basis. Antipasto is a mixture of salami, cheeses, olives and peppers. My oldest brother has continued this tradition of eating antipasto. He has a particular fondness for hot peppers. Not just peperoncini and Italian red peppers. The guy pops hard core peppers — serranos, cayennes, habaneros — like they're candy. As the youngest member of the family, I've had to endure his twisted sense of pepper-related humor for years at family gatherings. You'd think I'd learn my lesson by now, but I always seem to take the bait.

"Hmm," I'll say, examining a bowl of perfectly innocuous looking peppers. "Are these hot?"

"Those? No, they're very mild. Try one. You'll like 'em."

Ever the trusting little brother, I pop a whole pepper into my mouth. Five seconds later, my blistered mouth is burning beneath the kitchen faucet. I spend the remainder of the family dinner nursing the third-degree burns inside my mouth, contemplating legal action, while my brother falls all over himself cracking up.

Then there's Wren, who has an aversion to all things spicy. A bell pepper is too hot for her. I can't even sneak mild salsa into her burrito for fear she'll accuse me of domestic violence. At Thai restaurants, when a waiter asks her how hot she wants her food on a scale of one to ten, Wren has to use negative numbers. Before she orders at a new restaurant, she inquires as to the location of the nearest fire extinguisher. We're a ton of fun at Mexican and Indian restaurants.

Which can be a real drag since we have a lot of Indian friends who are kind enough to invite us into their homes for meals. The great thing is that most of them are vegetarians. The downside is that Wren believes most of these "friends" are trying to kill her.

Unlike my naïveté with my warped brother, Wren's taste

buds are hypersensitive. Whenever we receive an invitation for dinner at an Indian friend's home, I offer a feeble kind of disclaimer, which, by now, is practically scripted.

"We'd love to come to dinner. Um,...but, you know... my wife kind of has a problem with spicy foods," I say, hoping not to make presumptions about their food.

"No problem," they assure me. "Instead of adding fifteen Kashmir peppers, we'll only add twelve! How's that?"

"Works for me!"

At least I can tell Wren I tried.

But now, thanks to my encounter with Doctor Quack, I've figured out a way to address the issue without throwing my wife under the bus. From now on, whenever family or friends invite us to dinner, I can politely inform them: Oh, by the way, I can't eat spicy foods. Doctor's orders.

It's at least partly true. And it might save us both a trip to the burn unit at the hands of well-meaning friends or my sadistic brother.

DREAMING ON THE SEVENTH FLOOR

FOR JOHN LENNON, THE INTERSECTION at West 72nd Street and Central Park West was a portal to another world. Stepping out of the door of the Dakota Apartments, crossing Central Park West, and heading east into the park, John entered into his own Arcadia. A green world where he could ramble anonymously, dwarfed beneath the immensity of ancient oaks. A world alive with nature's rhythms, yet charged with the electrical energy of The City, where taxi horns harmonize with squawking birds and howling children. A world of wonder so teeming with the humming buzz of humanity that no one has time to gawk at a celebrity.

After years of flapping in the whirlwind of Beatlemania, it was this world in which John Lennon finally felt free. In this world, far from the Strawberry Fields of his childhood Liverpool, John Lennon found home.

For a month during the summer of 1978, it was also where I found home. While performing in a play at Theater for the New City in the East Village, I lived in room 710 on the seventh floor of the Olcott Hotel. John lived directly next door, on the seventh floor of The Dakota. Speaking strictly for myself, I was in seventh heaven. Not only was I getting paid to perform, I received a weekly per diem, and my stay at the Olcott Hotel was subsidized by our theatre company. My brief acting career never got any better than that. For that brilliant month, I was living the dream.

Lennon was living his own dream. Since the birth of his son, Sean, three years earlier, John had relished the role of househusband. Removed from the limelight of the rock and roll fantasy, John found his reality in baking bread, cooking rice, and playing with three-year-old Sean. Having been raised for most of his childhood separated from his own parents, John at last found the simple life he had dreamed of since he was a lad in Liverpool.

It was widely reported during this phase of his life that John had become a recluse, that he spent all of his time ensconced within the lavish walls of The Dakota, and that he rarely stepped outside. But John loved New York, his chosen city, and with Central Park mere steps from his front door, he spent far more time in the park than rock journalists documented. Legendary are the stories of folks who encountered John meandering down quiet pathways in the park, walking hand in hand with Yoko or with Sean. Most New Yorkers, inured to celebrity, never ventured a second glance at the Beatle who walked among them. But those astonished passersby who did say hello were rewarded with a shy smile and a warm greeting from John, just like he was a regular bloke.

During that magical month, I padded down every path within a square mile of The Dakota in search of John Lennon. As I crossed 72nd Street on my way to the subway, I would glance over my shoulder in the direction of The Dakota, hoping to pick out John among the multitudes. I imagined a scenario in which he would recognize me as a kindred spirit, and on discovering we were neighbors, would invite me over for tea. Sadly, I never caught a glimpse of my working class hero.

But late at night, I was reminded that John and I were separated by only a couple thin walls. So I would pick up my guitar and strum some old Beatles chestnut, imagining John was singing the same song at the same time, and that our voices rose beyond the walls to a place where our harmonies could be heard only by saints and angels. I imagined that our minds were on the same wavelength, receptive to the same creative ideas in the fertile firmament of Manhattan. It was the closest I ever got to a Beatle.

* * *

Today, when I cross that intersection at 72nd Street on my way to visit the mosaic memorial called Strawberry Fields, I still conjure an image of John crossing the street, holding firmly to Sean's hand; father and son, on a quiet stroll through the park. And I imagine a world in which John Lennon lives to a ripe old age, free to wander the meandering paths of Central Park without fear. In some future incarnation where there's nothing to kill or die for.

If I had seen John Lennon that summer, out in the park, or at the intersection of 72nd and Central Park West, I would have been too shy to interrupt him and too respectful of his privacy to offer even a simple hello. And even though we never met, for one brief moment in time we occupied the same space during some of the best nights of our lives. A visionary musician and a young actor, dreaming on the seventh floor of the greatest city in the world.

HOW I BEAT THE DRAFT

FORTY-FIVE YEARS AGO, I NEARLY became a soldier. Had I been born a few months earlier, I could have ended up in Vietnam, and returned a different person. Recently, my cousin Kathy asked me how I avoided getting drafted. I told her it was karma. The stars were aligned. The gods were watching over me. Serendipity smiled. Because just five months before I turned eighteen, the draft ended. For that fortuitous twist of fate, I am eternally grateful to every deity that ever swirled in the celestial sphere.

Before you think me unpatriotic, let me assure you: I love my country. But I never would have been able to cut it in the military. If there was some kind of alternative, I would have gladly accepted the opportunity to serve. However, out of the thousands of scruffy misfits in America during the seventies, I would have been one of the sorriest excuses for a solider in modern history.

See, I'm not what you'd call a model of virility. At the peak of my physical prowess, I weighed a hundred and thirty-five pounds and possessed an embarrassing lack of upper body strength. I suck at sports and I lack aggression. My only physical skill is my ability to run away from stuff. Regrettably, I've never been fast enough to outrun bullets. Guns terrify me. I don't think I even owned a squirt gun as a kid. When we played Cowboys and Indians, I was always the Indian who was tied to a tree and promptly forgotten.

In a hostage situation, I would be in familiar territory, but in combat I would be useless.

Then there's the fact that from age sixteen on, I was a vegetarian pacifist. In case you're unfamiliar with that phrase, let me translate it for you: coward. I've made a career out of avoiding physical confrontations, opting instead to reason my way out of conflicts — to employ the gentle art of persuasion that I developed in high school public speaking. If that doesn't work, I beg for mercy. As a last resort, I run like hell.

With the inexorable approach of my eighteenth birthday, I had to face the reality that I was a lover, not a fighter. I could make love (though my girlfriend might have disagreed), but not war. If love was all you need to be a soldier, I might have helped to win the war. But from what I saw on the nightly news, love was not all you need. You needed an M16 rifle. And an attitude.

Both of my older brothers were issued deferments, classified 4F. My brother Dennis explained to the induction psychiatrist that he was gay. In those days, military strategists were convinced that gay soldiers could concentrate on only one thing: how cute the enemy looked in those darling uniforms. When I heard what Dennis had done, I held out hope that I too could avoid the draft by telling the psychiatrist I was gay. But no matter how hard I tried, military uniforms never looked cute to me.

There was always Canada. I had a buddy who owned a VW Bus. We concocted a plan to sneak over the border from Washington into British Columbia and be genuine draft dodgers. But as a person who wears a sweatshirt to the beach, I knew I'd freeze to death in the frigid temperatures of Canada. Besides, I don't speak the language in British Columbia.

My fall back position was the priesthood. Priests were exempt from military service. Having been an altar boy, I had already given this vocation some serious consideration. But as every Catholic kid knows, in order to become a priest you must have a calling. God has to speak to you and let His will be known. At sixteen, the only thing speaking to me was my hormones. The idea of leading a life of celibacy held about as much interest for me as military uniforms.

The reality of the draft began to creep in each year as I sat around with my family eating Jiffy Pop while watching the annual draft lottery. The draft lottery had nothing to do with the NBA — though it did involve some of the top college prospects. It was a nationally televised event in which 366 capsules containing every birthdate in the calendar were put into a clear cylinder. Then they were drawn out, one by one, and announced to the viewing public. They tried to make it look fun, like it was a bingo game. Only the winner was the one whose number was called last. If your number was one of the first 215 numbers drawn, you were required to report for military induction within three months. Bingo!

Every year, I watched the lottery with detached curiosity. But as my eighteenth birthday approached in 1973, the lottery was no longer something abstract that I could view from the sidelines. Next year, I would be a participant.

During the spring of my senior year, I was selected to sing in the State High School Honor Choir. One Saturday morning in May, several members of my high school choir boarded a bus and headed for the Civic Auditorium in cosmopolitan Stockton. (Inexplicably, every major metropolis in California passed on this once-in-a-lifetime opportunity to put their city on the map. To this day, the artistic community in San Francisco bemoans its lack of vision for rejecting four hundred adolescent musical prodigies, who, without question, would have permanently altered the cultural landscape of The City.)

Once we arrived in Stockton, we rehearsed for several hours. After an hour of afternoon rehearsal, the bespectacled conductor of the State Honor Choir removed his glasses, and said he had an important announcement to make. He waited for silence, paused for effect, and cleared his throat. Then, in dramatic fashion, he proclaimed that he had just been informed that the draft for the Vietnam War would end on June 30th of that year.

A rapturous cheer built to a crescendo as four hundred singers rose as one body and erupted in the longest standing ovation I have ever witnessed. The room was a riot of ecstasy: Pimply-faced tenors and basses, rapidly approaching draft age, few of whom would have survived the Army, whooping and whistling. The sopranos and altos equally as jubilant, wrapping their arms around each other and jumping up and down. Everyone thrusting their arms toward the ceiling, stomping their feet, pounding their hands together thunderously.

Finally, after an eternity, the applause dissipated, and we sat back down. The next song that we sang was a miracle, sung in soulful harmony:

I'm gonna lay down my burden
Down by the riverside;
I'm gonna study war no more.

We celebrated the way we knew best, singing full-throated, investing the song with all the energy we'd been holding in reserve. Four hundred voices that would not be silenced by the dirge of war.

Until 1975, the Selective Service System went through the motions of still conducting draft lotteries. But no one paid much attention to them. No matter which numbers were called, no one was required to report to an induction center for a physical, or to boot camp; much less to Vietnam. The draft was over. And even though it was required by law that all young men register for the draft when they turned eighteen, it was never enforced. Still, the fact that I refused to register allowed me to think of myself as a rebel and a draft resistor.

As my values have solidified over the past forty-five years, I can now say with certainty that I object to war in all its forms on moral grounds. Thankfully, I'm too old to be drafted. But as a vegetarian pacifist conscientious objector, if my country ever needs me, I'm ready to serve. As long as they classify me 4H. That way, I can work with animals. And no matter where they station me, I can guarantee that no animals will be killed.

SINGING HARMONY

I WAS BORN THIS WAY. SINGING, I mean. I came out of the womb scatting in three-four time. The first sound I made wasn't a cry, it was an F sharp. Those tears streaming down my face weren't from sadness, they expressed the passion of my first spontaneous composition: *Take Me to My Crib.*

It must have been rough for my mother. When you have a child devoid of musical aptitude who sings all day like Little Richard with his hair on fire, it can be challenging. Throughout my childhood, Mom stifled the urge to tear out my vocal cords with her bare hands. But after years of enduring my incessant off-key screeching, she struck upon an ingenious method of silencing me.

For my eighth birthday, she bought me a black, plastic transistor radio. The radio wasn't much to look at—some off-brand Japanese model she purchased for a couple bucks at Woolworth's. It may have been cheap, but that sucker could pull in KLIV and KYA like a charm. Mom hoped that the professional off-key singers I heard on the radio would drown out my singing. How was she to know that I would sing along with every song? Even the crappy ones by Donnie Osmond.

By the time I was a teenager, I'd cycled through three or four transistor radios. My final transistor was totally trashed, held together with masking tape, until the day

117

I accidentally stepped on it, and reduced it to a pile of rubble. My transistor days were over. By that time I had amassed a vast data base of songs in my hippocampus that could be recalled at any time, note for note, like an iPod set to shuffle. Those songs travel with me to this day in my own personal "cloud," emerging spontaneously to serve as the soundtrack for whatever set of circumstances I find myself in. I don't need ear buds; the music's hardwired into my brain.

A few years ago I realized the music wasn't just inside my brain. One morning when I was in our school's staff room, running off some copies, my colleague, Johanna, observed, "You know, the great thing about you, is that you're always singing."

Oops. Did I sing that out loud? It's likely I've been singing out loud without knowing it my whole life. That might explain the peculiar looks I've gotten over the years. Perhaps I should seek professional help. There's this condition called Compulsive Singing Disorder I read about online. I have all of the classic symptoms, but I'm not too worried. That's a disorder I can live with. But what if it became contagious? What if it spread like a virus, so that people sang everywhere? In unison. In duets and quartets. On street corners with perfect strangers. In harmony for the whole world to hear. An epidemic like that would be hard to cure.

* * *

I once read about this remote village in India, where the people wake early every morning and sing until the sun comes up. Educated skeptics laugh at the ignorance of these unsophisticated people who don't understand the science behind the rising and setting of the sun. But the villagers point out that in all of the thousands of years that they and their ancestors have been singing, the sun has never once failed to rise.

Like these unsophisticated village people, I'm going to keep singing, my music on an endless loop like a mantra in my mind. I only hope my singing creates a little harmony and maybe helps the sun rise one more day. It hasn't failed me yet.

ACKNOWLEDGMENTS

Thanks to Bob Jenkins for forty years of inspiration, encouragement and friendship. You planted the seed for this book; hopefully a few more will bloom in the future. Thank you, Aaron Lee, for continually answering my technological questions. Thanks also to Glendon Haddix and his team at Streetlight Graphics for their outstanding, creative designs, assistance, and patience. Thanks most importantly to Wren who unfailingly loves and supports me. Sorry to make you the target of so many jokes, sweetie. But if I make fun of my brother too much, he'll beat me up.

BIOGRAPHY

Brian Conroy taught theatre, public speaking and storytelling for 35 years. He is the author of the children's book, *Prince Dighavu*. This is his first collection of essays.